Flying South

No. 7

2020

Managing Editor:	Steve Lindahl
Poetry Editor:	Mary Hennessy
Non-fiction Editor:	Jennifer Stevenson Vincent
Fiction Editor:	Bob Shar
Fiction Readers:	Ray Morrison Steve Lindahl

President's Favorite chosen by:
Bart Ganzert

Cover Art: Barbara Rizza Mellin

Flying South is a literary magazine/writing contest published annually by Winston-Salem Writers, an association of writers and readers with the purpose of:

Helping writers interact with other writers, improve their craft, and realize their goals.

Information about Winston-Salem Writers can be found at the website: **www.wswriters.org**

Winston-Salem Writers is a non-profit organization and a member of The Arts Council of Winston-Salem and Forsyth County, NC.

Contents

2020 Best in Category Winners:

Fiction:

Non-Fiction:

Poetry:

Kim Bonner

The Downtown Improvement Society

The representative from Mahan Investments saw none of the eccentric charm promised in the town's brochure.

Oak Street boasted a colorful past, including gunfights and hangings, all meticulously catalogued by the historical society. Once, LBJ had visited. As the story went, he was captivated by the itinerant preacher who stood on the corner every Wednesday, rain or shine, to spread the gospel. Mahan Investments knew nothing of the President's visit or the street preacher, or the preacher's son, who had proselytized on that very corner himself for years. He'd eventually succumbed to the apathy of his would-be parishioners and started a prison ministry.

With the departure of the preacher's son, downtown lost the last of its eccentrics. Back in the day, old man Puckett rode his horse down the sidewalk every afternoon at 2 p.m. sharp for the sole purpose of allowing the beast to relieve herself just outside the only pawnshop in town. The former cowhand had a bitter rivalry with the store's owner over a grievance so old neither of them remembered what it was about.

The men would scream at each other for a few minutes, after which Puckett prodded his ancient mare down the street and out of town. The storeowner would bluster and stew as he shoveled manure off the sidewalk while tourists snapped videos with their cell phones.

By the time the representative from Mahan Investments arrived, the storeowner had turned the keys over to the bank and moved to Ohio. Puckett outlived his horse by twelve days and was buried next to her with much fanfare. Oak Street was preacher and manure-free on the day the representative arrived to inspect three blocks of century-old buildings that might become the next Charleston or Wilmington. Or not.

"So as you can see, these historic buildings are just a treasure," said Marceline Hobart, listing agent, president of the

Downtown Improvement Society, and vice president of the Historical Society. She turned her wrist as if brandishing a wand while she spoke. Miss Marceline ran the Downtown Improvement Society with an iron fist and relentless optimism. Florid and heavyset, she teetered on her best pair of faux leather pumps like a plump bird trying to navigate walking in galoshes.

"This particular one was built in 1905. Upstairs was a dentist's office when I was a child. His patient chair is still up there. It would just be marvelous to have someone breathe new life into it."

"Is this knob and tube electric?" the man asked. He ran his fingers down the wiring panel, incredulous. "I don't think this is even legal."

Miss Marceline blustered on. "It needs updates, to be sure. But the bones! They just don't build like this anymore. This is solid brick!"

He shrugged. "It's brick façade maybe, but I'm more interested in what's behind it. What kind of roof is it?"

Her hand fluttered to her chest. "Why, it's, well, it's been through hurricanes and wars and recessions, and it's still on." She thrust her chin out a little. Bright pink lipstick bled into the cracks around her mouth.

"Looks like termite droppings over there."

"Well, the building can easily be tented. The owner next door hasn't got on board with splitting the cost yet," she said. "And, it's no good tenting part of the block and not the whole. Those little rascals will just come right back."

She flicked her hand at the offending insects. "That's why having it all under one owner would be marvelous." She added, "*Marvelous.*"

"So this whole block is all under one roof? Who owns the stairwells in between the buildings? Did the previous owners get a survey and title insurance? An inspection?"

The representative wiped his hand across his upper lip. Already sweating through his dress shirt, his throat had begun to close up a little when he inhaled the mold, dust and rodent droppings. Miss Marceline looked aghast at his questions. Beads of perspiration trickled down her fleshy bosom.

"Everyone uses the stairwells. These buildings don't have elevators. You can't *own* a stairwell."

"Are you sure you're a licensed realtor?"

* * *

The second representative brought with him an engineer and a tape measurer. Miss Marceline trundled down the street in sweltering heat and humidity to give them the grand tour. Again. She wore pantyhose and a crisp white blazer over a peach floral dress, her ample hips swaying to and fro as she gesticulated in front of each building, listing the endless retail possibilities. A coffee shop! Perhaps an ice cream parlor or a bookstore or another antique store. No wine bistros, though. The Downtown Improvement Society members were Baptists.

"These were built to last. Just look at the wood."

She ran her hand over the wall panel, picking up a thick film of dust. As the two men shone penlights onto the ceiling and into the corners, she discreetly dug in her purse for a tissue to wipe away the offending grime. A window AC unit kicked on, rattling in protest at being called into service. The store was littered with bric-a-brac, chipped teacups, old school desks and naked Barbies.

"Solid wood!" she reminded them.

"I appreciate this is heavy timber construction, ma'am, but we're concerned with the level of dry rot and water damage. You leave these old buildings untended for too long, and—"

The engineer received a rebuke in the form of Miss Marceline waving a tissue in front of his face. "The Downtown Improvement Society tends just fine, thank you."

"Let's go upstairs," the second representative said. "It used to be a medical office."

"Dentist," Miss Marceline corrected him. "Dr. Brevard. A wonderful man."

The engineer looked around the store. "So the stairs are?"

"Outside. Street entrance. Second-floor landing connects to the other building, which is not currently for sale," the second representative said.

"Not for sale *yet*," Miss Marceline corrected him. "We just need to sweet talk the owner a bit. He's a tough nut. He goes to the *other* Baptist church."

"Who owns the stairwell?" the engineer asked.

"Apparently, no one," the second representative said.

Outside, the humidity wafted over and through them, sapping away any coolness the air condition had provided. While Miss Marceline fumbled with a large set of keys, the engineer tugged at his shirt collar, trying to release trapped body heat.

"What's that smell?" the second representative asked.

"Juice plant. This is citrus country. Maybe you can open up one of those custom smoothie places using local produce? Wouldn't that be *marvelous*?" She triumphantly opened the wrought-iron gate and they ascended the stairwell.

"Smells like feet," the engineer mumbled.

They stepped around broken glass and ducked underneath a jerry-rigged lighting system that was strung from corner to corner.

"The owner was going to put apartments up here. You can see he started to frame it out. But he got sick, lung cancer, poor thing, and they moved back to Savannah," Miss Marceline said.

"Probably asbestos poisoning." The engineer pulled his shirt collar over his nose.

"Why is the floor so squishy?" the second representative asked.

"Rotted joist," the engineer replied.

"It feels fine to me," Miss Marceline said at the same time.

The men whispered, took some notes, dabbed handkerchiefs behind their necks. Looked closer into the corners and choked back coughs as the fetid air finally become intolerable.

"I have to be honest, ma'am, this looks like an EPA mitigation project to me. At best, it's a teardown," the engineer said.

Miss Marceline drew back as if she'd been slapped by her very own grandma. "*Teardown*? Over my dead body."

She ran her hand across the patient chair, its frame rusted and leather cushion eaten through by rodents. "This is living history." She raised her right index finger in the air, a signal to all who knew her that Marceline Hobart was about to speak the truth and you better by God start listening.

"Dr. Brevard was the only dentist in town, the only one for sixty miles back when sixty miles might as well have been five hundred. He never turned anyone away, even if they had no money. We could put up a tribute plaque." She wagged her finger at the men. "This building is the *heart* of our town." To punctuate the sentiment, she folded her hands over her heart, just as she'd taught her Sunday school class to do when signing the words to "Jesus Loves Me."

The engineer was nonplussed. "This whole building is canted. You can just look at the exterior walls and see—"

"McCrory's Five and Dime was across the street. That building is also for sale. We have the original sign at the historical society. I'm the vice president." The pitch of her voice rose to a squeak. Settling for vice president had been a bitter pill to swallow but how could she have known that Sadie Hewitt would start campaigning for president so early in the year?

"See that crack?" The engineer pointed above a window, missing most of its glass and patched with a garbage bag. "That's probably structural. Means the foundation is damaged."

Miss Marceline wheezed. The second representative tucked a memo pad back into his shirt pocket and cleared his throat while the engineer rattled off a damage report. Extensive dry rot. Metal plates on exterior walls indicating the buildings had been reinforced at some point, and maybe not so well. Uncooperative neighbors. And that's even before the roof inspection.

Miss Marceline slumped, her linen jacket now a bundle of wrinkles as he made his case for the owners to cut their losses and get out. While the engineer spoke, her jacket sprouted large stains under the armpits. When he reached the topic of architectural salvage and the minimal value the building's "artifacts" would bring to the finished project, her eyes fluttered shut. Maybe, thought the second representative aloud, there was potential to market the downtown as a reproduction. Like a less authentic Colonial Williamsburg. What kind of deal could be made?

She lovingly caressed the dentist's chair even as her jaw tightened and moisture crept down her back. "Nothing gets demolished. These buildings are alive with history."

"Ma'am, these buildings are alive with airborne pathogens and fire hazards," the engineer said, not unkindly. "They can't be saved. I'm actually amazed they're still standing. We can build better ones with exactly the same appearance. With central air and elevators."

Marceline's front teeth gleamed with the pink Revlon hue she'd chewed off her lower lip. "No demolition. I can throw in the original furnishings," she whispered. "That's my final offer."

* * *

Despite the gloomy field report, a third representative materialized with a flashy PowerPoint presentation to the city council. They sent it to staff for review and recommendations.

Meanwhile, Marceline pressed on. She briskly rejected applications to change exterior facades. When a fledgling farm-to-table restaurant applied for a liquor license, she gave a rousing speech in opposition when it came before the city council.

"I think we are being short-sighted here," said one of the newer members. Marceline particularly despised him because he had moved to town less than two years earlier and immediately begun dispensing advice based on how they did things back in New Jersey.

"It would bring people downtown. Isn't that what we want?" the councilman asked.

"We want the right kind of people," she replied.

The vote was deferred pending staff's report on the Mahan Group's proposal. The third representative had been brought in to charm the officials and members of the Downtown Improvement Society. Tall and courtly, he had a soft drawl, which was affected, and wore cowboy boots purchased the week before. Splashy color graphics accompanied his homespun presentation. One of the council members discreetly powdered her nose as he spoke.

Marceline twisted the agenda in her hands. No way, no how. She had the votes sewn up, she was sure. All but that pesky Yankee. The Downtown Improvement Society was poised to give an impassioned defense of the proud old buildings that just needed a bit of love to bring them back to life. She narrowed her eyes as the third representative wrapped up his talk to a smattering of polite applause. When she rose to speak, someone tugged on her sleeve.

"Marceline. Since I am the incoming president, I think it best for me to speak," said Sadie Hewitt.

"But I—I'm still in charge until next Tuesday," Marceline sputtered.

Sadie gave her a soft smile. "We already decided, honey. You weren't able to make the meeting last month, remember?"

"It was my granddaughter's birthday. I only get to see her a few times a year."

"Still. You weren't there and we voted…on several things. It's my turn to speak now."

Still nattering protests, Marceline was gently guided back to her seat by a fellow society member. The others avoided eye contact with her.

"This is not protocol." She sniffed in irritation and looked at one of the council members, an avid preservationist. The woman would not return her gaze. Marceline began to scrape her front teeth against her lower lip.

"It is a difficult thing, to admit when things are too far gone to fix," Sadie began. Marceline's mouth dropped.

"We must concur that the structural damage is too extensive to repair. Our only option is to rebuild with our new partners and go forward into a new era. Unfortunately, the past, in this case, cannot be preserved, but it can be remembered and reconstructed better than it ever was. On behalf of the Society, I offer our wholehearted endorsement to this proposal."

"No!" Marceline lumbered to her feet, like an angry mama bear defending her cub against poachers. "That is *not* what I—we—decided. Traitors!"

The chair banged his gavel and demanded order.

"Public comment on this proposal will be at the end of the meeting, Ms. Hobart. You are a member of the public, just like everyone else, so wait your turn," he said, not without a glint of satisfaction in his eye.

"This isn't happening! I am still in charge of the Society. *You.*" She jabbed a finger at Sadie. "You just sit down and shut up!" An index finger was raised. Time to deliver some truth telling. No one crossed her. No one. She paused to soak in the moment as she, Marceline Larose Hobart, war bride, widow, dowager queen, singlehandedly fought back the interlopers who would defile her town.

But instead of obedient silence there were gasps, a few chuckles, and eyes that seemed piteous, not chastened. The whispers floated past her ears as she stood like a mannequin, finger still pointed skyward. *This is why we had a quorum vote without her, poor thing. Past her prime. We had to drop her as the listing agent.*

Another bang of the gavel.

"I will order you removed if you don't sit down," the chair said, not even bothering to hide his triumphant grin.

She slumped in her chair, waving off a plastic cup of water someone offered her. Mute with fury, her eyes darted back and forth as Sadie wrapped up her comments. Then some of the merchants spoke, followed by owners who had purchased at the nadir of the real estate market hoping to flip the buildings, realizing too late they were in over their heads.

"Personally, I'd rather have these folks buy us out instead of letting the banks foreclose. They're gonna pour a whole bunch of money in this town, even build an open space for the kids to play. We have to move on," the owner of the old McCrory's building said. "All of us."

"Traitor," Marceline croaked.

When her turn came, she strode to the podium and raised a balled-up fist in the air.

"Your comment card, please," said the city clerk.

"Why? Wha—you all know who I am."

"It's for recordkeeping ma'am. Please fill out the card," the chair said.

Flushed, Marceline scratched her name on one of the pre-printed cards. Only the sound of the second hand on the wall clock could be heard as she signed with a flourish.

"Now then, let's get some things straight," she began.

There was money available for restoration. Federal money. Private grants. No, she hadn't applied for any yet. Yes, there was *some* termite damage. No, there had not been any other offers. Yes, it's true she had personally rejected 80% of the requests made to the Society for matters as small as changing the color of an awning. When the timer dinged after three minutes, she haughtily returned to her seat. A scent trailed behind her, an indistinguishable mélange of drugstore talc, hairspray, and a long discontinued brand of perfume she found on auction sites.

The vote was unanimous in favor of the Mahan Group's proposal. With a flourish, the council chair initialed the demolition permit.

"This is the beginning of a long and prosperous friendship," he said to the third representative, whose too-tight cowboy boots had already begun to rub blisters on his heels.

"Over my dead body!" Marceline screamed, causing more than a few snickers.

While the attendees filed out, shaking hands and studiously avoiding eye contact with the erstwhile grande dame, the third representative furtively slipped out of his boots and into a pair of Italian loafers. Neutered and without a title for the first time in three decades, Marceline lurched to her Buick where she slumped over the steering wheel and sobbed inconsolably.

Never one to dwell on her feelings, she righted herself after thirty minutes and reapplied lipstick by light of the visor mirror. An action plan began forming in her mind even as she blotted with a tattered Kleenex. Over the following weeks, while posters and billboards announcing the arrival of the Mahan Group sprouted up around town, Marceline busied herself preparing the necessary paperwork to obtain an injunction.

* * *

Every lawyer in town and two towns over refused to take the case. *Cowards.* Lawyers on the other coast refused even a free initial consultation, reasoning that Mahan Investments was a juggernaut no one dared impede. They would mire you in paperwork, run up the litigation costs so high that no one could afford to take them on. Once they got their hooks into a town, paid for all the shiny new playgrounds and civic centers, they were like a bad rash you couldn't excise even with a scalpel. Everything came at a cost. One of the lawyers summed it up before hanging up brusquely.

"This is the future, ma'am. You have to take the bad with the good. These old towns are dying on the vine. Let some new blood have a chance pruning them and see what grows back."

Traitors.

She pressed on, spending every waking hour at the cramped law library reading moldy treatises on property law, going over the city's zoning code with a fine tooth comb, and hand-writing letters to the editor. The paper politely declined to run her submissions, but surely, the judge would see reason. She had taught him in Sunday school, after all. No one stepped across from Marceline Hobart and came out unscathed.

On the Saturday that was to have been the groundbreaking, Oak Street stood, as usual, silent and empty. Before a packed courtroom on Friday, the judge had issued an emergency stay halting the demolition and construction. Afterward, Miss Marceline clutched the signed ruling to her chest like a prized possession that had been lost and re-discovered. Eye rolls and scowls followed her as she heaved down the courthouse stairs, stopping to catch her breath every few steps. The third representative, cowboy boots nowhere in sight, huddled with the company's attorney outside discussing the cost of appeal versus the cost of abandoning the project. Miss Marceline made her way to Dr. Brevard's office and dropped into his exam chair. Through the broken windows, a slight breeze carried wafts of citrus and pigeon droppings, mixed with burnt marijuana from the squatters living across the street.

With the winter season approaching, the snowbirds, annual visitors fleeing the harsh northern winter, would return, maybe hoping to put down roots or buy an investment property. Perhaps a historic building in small-town America would be right up their alley. A downtown resurgence was just around the corner. Miss Marceline was sure of it. First they'd restore one building, then another, then another. When her chest let out a death rattle, she was smiling. The people would come. It was going to be marvelous.

Emily Wilmer

California Dementia

Fires, something to do with fires.
Are there fires? Was it a dream
or are there fires?

There were fires last year
but no fires now.

There was a fire.
The house burned down.

Do you know how I met John?
We met as teachers.

You told me once
but tell me again.

What did you say about fires?
Are there fires? Was it a dream?

Not to worry.
There are no fires.

Did you know John taught math?
I taught P.E.

I think there was a fire.
The house burned down and
my doll burned up
with the house.

Did I tell you how I met John?

I love that story of
how you met John.
Tell me again.

Claire Thomas

Lehinch

The BMW hummed down the M50 towards Galway. Occasionally, I imagined the EuroCar sticker on the back windshield was gone, and, for a split second, this rental was my own. The first hour and a half of the drive was sunny and pleasant enough that I had forgotten I was driving on the opposite side of the road, and on the opposite side of the car. Once I exited for Limerick and proceeded westward, the clouds changed. The sky grew dark and the telephone lines whipped and furled at the wind's mercy. Fields alongside the motorway had flooded and my windshield wipers couldn't keep pace with the golf ball-sized raindrops plummeting from the sky. The roads were more narrow than they had been in Dublin. I drove slowly, trying not to wince at every approaching car despite the drivers being close enough I could give a high-five in passing.

I finally reached Lehinch, a coastal village along Ireland's Wild Atlantic Way. The car violently shook against the wind as I approached the sea and coasted into town. In an effort to strategically park as to avoid the seemingly inevitable topple of the many, swaying telephone poles, I made a few laps around the town center. The fear of totaling the shiny, borrowed BMW was palpable. I parked and walked towards the Lehinch Hostel, indicated by a blunt sign stating "Enter". The wall of wind buckled my knees as I leaned into it. Cold and wet, it slapped me to the point of disorientation. My hair proved to be a nemesis as it coiled around my face, pelting me in the cheeks and sheeting my eyes while my long, impractical-yet-fashionable coat billowed behind me, creating a wind-catching parachute of sorts. I would soon find out that I arrived in Lehinch the same day as Storm Jorge.

The hostel was simple and damp but I had a room to myself and a view of the ocean from my window. The windowsill was wide enough to sit on and I spent some time looking out at the sea. The water was grey and angry. White caps from hundreds of feet away roared to shore in a cold fury. I called my mother to assure her I was alive. "My Irish friend Aileen told me that mental illness is rampant in Western Ireland. The daily winds drive the residents insane, or drive them to drink" she proceeded to tell me. I continued my gaze across the water, "I don't blame them".

The sea seemed to snarl with a particular moodiness, hammering its weight into the streets of town. I wanted to walk around, but I had finally gotten warm in the confides of my room and wasn't keen on getting voluntarily pummeled yet again so I decided to sit by the window and watch the town from there. I watched the waves crash into the rocks and send sea foam high into the air. Like weightless balls of cotton, it floated through the alleyways and streets. From my windowsill, it almost looked like snow.

I heard the soft strum of a guitar drift from the next room, and, in brief moments when the wind wasn't wailing at my window, singing. I had woken up early that morning and the day's drive was unnerving so I began to feel tired. I climbed into the top bunk and nestled myself underneath the heavy, wool comforter. I listened to the relentless wind rip through the streets accompanied by the acoustic guitar. In a town of wind-driven maniacs and peculiar snowfall, I was lulled to sleep.

Elizabeth Tarver

Nemesis

Harriet found it difficult to listen to the Trinket Man as he prattled on about the North Carolina souvenirs he was selling. She kept looking at her watch. It was nearly two in the afternoon. Her son would be getting out of school soon.

"I bet you never seen this before," the Trinket Man said, flashing his grin of crooked coffee-stained teeth. He had tattoos all up and down his arms. Purple and red and black ones. Devilish looking things. On one arm, the lines wove in and out and met to form a plump pulsating heart, complete with bulging blue veins. *Soul Prison*, it said. On the other arm, a woman's slender leg peeked out from beneath his short-sleeved shirt. Harriet guessed there was a naked woman hiding under the fabric. Probably buxom and brunette like Erica, the woman who'd be picking up her son from school. Erica, her ex-husband's live-in girlfriend, the tattooed woman with the Bettie Page hairdo, the vintage clothes, and the killer figure. Harriet felt a sinking feeling in her stomach. The old familiar feeling of regret, jealousy, and resentment. She hated the sight of tattoos.

"Well, have ya?"

"Have I what?" Harriet found herself looking into the Trinket Man's eyes. They were bright and open wide. He wanted her to buy these things. He was desperate.

"A hillbilly outhouse. It's made of genuine North Carolina pine." He held a miniature wooden outhouse in his hand. *North Carolina* was scrawled in cursive print across the door under the crescent moon cutout. "Look here. The door even has tiny little hinges. It's a working door. Can you beat it?"

"I think we better stick to mugs and magnets."

"Oh, come on now, y'all need to expand. You can do better than this." He scrunched up his nose and, with a wave of his hand, dismissed the small souvenir section of Ayres' U-Pick-It Farm.

"I just don't think hillbilly outhouses are nice. Our customers aren't looking for bathroom humor."

"Hillbillies are in, darlin'. Haven't you been watching reality TV? Hillbillies are taking over show biz. That's where items like the hillbilly outhouse come in. You ought to capitalize before the buzz ends."

"That's enough," Harriet said. She did not like being called darling. "No outhouses. Not now. Not ever. Carolina cardinal mugs, some NC State key chains – that's all fine and good – but I draw the line at hillbilly humor. We are not hillbillies at the U-Pick-It.

"I never said you was," the Trinket Man protested, his voice ringing with sarcasm. He stuffed the little outhouse back in its box and then shoved it into a bigger box. "You don't have to be ugly about it."

Harriet watched the tattooed heart grow larger as the Trinket Man forced open another box and pulled out a mug depicting an idealized Smoky Mountains scene – pale blue hills contrasting with an orange sky at sunset. "Why do you have those tattoos?" she blurted out.

"You don't like my tattoos? Is that why you never buy nothing but mugs?"

"No," Harriet said. "I'd just like to know what motivates people to get tattoos. Why'd you do it?"

"Same reason people put bumper stickers on their cars, I guess. It's how I say who I am. These are who I am," he said, rubbing his arms. "I got more on my back. You want to see them?"

"Absolutely not," Harriet said.

"Ok, but I'm telling you y'all need to expand this souvenir section. A store like this needs more than just mugs and magnets and cornhusk dolls. Damn passé if you ask me."

* * *

Twenty years ago Harriet's uncle Hal came up with the idea of turning the family farm into a U-Pick-It operation. They weren't very good tobacco farmers, having failed repeatedly to control a nasty case of tobacco mosaic virus, and so they sold some of the Ayres acreage they'd inherited to raise funds. Harriet's great-grandfather, Frank Ayres, who they called Papa, was still alive at the time, and they hid the land sales from him.

"Why is there a trailer on the lower forty? There's some shabby-looking people milling around there too. And what is that fat boy doing riding a four-wheeler on our land?" Papa began to ask questions and to placate him, they made up stories.

"We're hiring some folks to help out, Papa," they'd say. "It's just temporary."

"Well, I hope you're not paying them too much. You can't count on people like that. They run off at the most crucial times. Not that I want them there in the first place."

The farm and its adjoining lands had been in the family since before the Civil War. The Ayres had grown tobacco there for well over a hundred years. Generation after generation of Ayres had planted, sold, and smoked it. Papa liked to say that the soil was full of salty Ayres sweat and that the salt was like a poison, working its way up through the tobacco and stunting it. The more you worked the less the land responded. This was the farmer's lament, he said on the front porch of the old farmhouse where he'd been born and now lived with Uncle Hal and Aunt Lydia, to his chagrin. He'd sit in a low cowhide rocker, his knees level with his chest and he'd smoke a pipe filled with his own Ayres tobacco. Every once in a while, he'd swat at Harriet's cousins, all of whom were younger than she, with a plastic fly swatter.

"Steer clear. Back it up," he growled. His feet were tender and the cousins were apt to tread on them if they got too close.

"Get away from Papa," Harriet would join in, lunging at the cousins until they scattered.

Harriet and her parents lived across the road in a tiny brick house her father had built with her mother's small inheritance. It wasn't much but it gave them distance from the farmhouse, which had become overcrowded when Uncle Hal married Aunt Lydia and began begetting all the cousins.

"Do something about these heathens, Lydia," Papa would yell, and Aunt Lydia would seethe, her plump face turning bright red.

"I've told Hal he needs to go to a nursing home. He's too much to handle."

It was true that Papa was obstinate and headstrong. He sat every day on the porch whether there was sunshine or rain, whether it was hot or cold, and he gazed out half-blind at his fields. In the winter, they bundled him up in blankets and placed earmuffs on him. He refused to come inside, even in the bleakest weather, until it was suppertime.

"I can't for the life of me understand why he hasn't gotten pneumonia," Aunt Lydia grumbled one cold winter day as she fixed him lunch on a tray. It was a Saturday, and Harriet always took Papa his lunch tray when she wasn't in school.

"Papa isn't ever going to die," Harriet said. "I'll be grown up with kids of my own, and he'll still be sitting there."

"That wouldn't surprise me one bit," Aunt Lydia snapped, shoving the lunch tray into Harriet's hands.

* * *

Aunt Lydia said the U-Pick-It farm needed a trinket shop, as she called it. "Something cute, where we can sell jam and pickles and little souvenirs." Harriet was only eleven at the time, and it sounded wonderful. She imagined an endless supply of candy. The thought of the gang of cousins tearing through the store bothered her, but she tried to put it out of her mind.

The little store went up quickly, and it wasn't long before the vegetables and blueberries were growing. Harriet's father decided it would be nice to have another seasonal business to keep things going in the winter so they planted Christmas trees as well.

At first Papa didn't notice and then one day, as they were driving to church, he bellowed, "Where's the tobacco? And what is that building doing over yonder?"

"That's our new store, Papa," Harriet's mother said. She was the only cynic in the family. She'd never been supportive of the U-Pick-It idea, and most of all she hated the lies they told Papa.

"Barbara!" Harriet's father tensed at the steering wheel.

"Our new what?"

"You really need to tell him the truth, Dwight."

Harriet was sitting in the back seat with Papa. She saw his eyes water.

"What have you done with our farm?"

"It's still our farm, Papa. We just had to change it some. You know how we had trouble with that virus. And besides, tobacco causes cancer. We have to plan for the future."

"Damned do-gooders ruined the tobacco industry with all that cancer talk. I been smoking all my life and look at me – fit as a fiddle." Papa followed this with a bout of coughing and wheezing.

"Maybe so, but the fact is we had to make a change."

"Is that corn I see?" Papa sat erect and squinted his eyes, peering hard into the distance. Harriet squinted too and tried to imagine Papa's world in which everything was blurry and hazy. Things were rarely as they seemed, and change came crashing down abruptly like an avalanche on a nature show.

"Yes, sir."

"That corn's as tall as a man. How long has this been going on under my nose?"

On the way to church that day, Harriet's father made a full confession and to their surprise, Papa was pleased.

"Could be change is just what this place needs," he said. "Anyone who talks about the good old days is talking a bunch of lies."

"Yes, sir," Harriet's father said and he shot Harriet's mother a triumphal glance.

"Aren't you mad about all the lies you were told?" she asked.

Papa ignored her and opined about planting muscadine grapes, which he knew for a fact young children love to eat straight from the vine. "Attracts wasps, though. That's the downside. Leave it to these kids today to get stung and come whining about it. In my day, we didn't bat an eyelash if we got wasp-stung. All we cared about was getting that sugar off the vine."

A week later, Papa died in his sleep. Heart failure, they whispered, as the funeral home came for the body. When no one was looking, Harriet took his pipe from his nightstand and stuffed it in her pocket. A few days later when Uncle Hal asked where it was, she lied and said she didn't know. It was under her bed in a shoebox.

* * *

It sometimes seemed that the years had sprouted wings and flown off like a startled flock of birds. Harriet had graduated from high school and community college. She'd even gotten married. Still, she judged that her life had been a monotonous routine of futile and meaningless activities until she was offered a position at a bank in Raleigh. It wasn't long before she'd become overly familiar with her co-worker, Carlton Hepplewhite. It was wrong and her husband William would have been furious, but Carlton was dapper-looking in his wool suits and regimental striped ties. She liked it when he wore the pink and green striped tie with the matching hankie square for his coat pocket. His shoes were always shiny wing tips, but in the summer, he wore white bucks and seersucker suits with bow ties in the colors of rainbow sherbet.

She spent all her lunch breaks with Carlton. Where they went didn't matter, as long as she was with him. Sometimes, she tagged along and watched him get a haircut at the barbershop. Harriet marveled at Carlton's perfect hair, the way it parted on the side and was never out of place. Other times, they drove to various menswear stores while Carlton tried on suits and sports coats. Harriet liked to pick out the ties. William never wore ties. Once she picked out a pair of cufflinks that Carlton loved. They were enamel with navy and gold stripes.

"Your wife certainly has good taste," the salesman said. Carlton winked at Harriet and pinched her cheek.

"You bet she does," he said. "That's why I bring her along."

If they got back to the bank early enough, they'd sit in Carlton's BMW and hold hands. They never ate lunch since Carlton was careful about his weight, and they never kissed. Harriet guessed that Carlton didn't want to kiss her because she was married. Or else he simply didn't like kissing.

At the end of the day, William would drive up to the bank in his pickup truck and walk in covered in dust or mud from a construction site where he was working. Harriet always turned red when William showed up. She couldn't tell whether she was embarrassed about the way William looked or the fact that William and Carlton were in the same building. The man she was married to and the man she adored were two different people. It was discombobulating.

One rainy spring day, Carlton took her on a drive through the Hayes Barton neighborhood in Raleigh, and they looked at the million dollar homes made of substantial brick or stone. There was one with a green tile roof and a front porch. Dogwoods bloomed all over the yard.

"Now that's what you call gracious living," Carlton said. "I can see us there. Me on the front porch swing. You bringing me a glass of lemonade. I would wear my cable knit cardigan – the white one with the navy stripe – and you . . . ." Carlton paused and gazed at her. He grabbed her hand and held it. "You'd be in a pink cashmere sweater set with a pearl necklace, patterned Capri pants, ballet flats – I saw some at Dillard's, by the way, and you'd look great in them. You've got such tiny feet."

"Would we have kids, Carlton?"

"Kids? Of course. I'd prefer twins. Twin boys. They'd be dressed just like me but in different colored cardigans. Baby blue and lime green maybe. They'd definitely be holding tennis rackets. But maybe lime green is too feminine? Maybe we should go with Kelly green instead."

"No, lime green is perfect."

Carlton leaned over and, for the first time, kissed her on the cheek. She felt warm and full of shivers at the same time. Her eyes filled with tears.

When she was back behind the teller counter, she tried to pretend nothing had happened. William picked her up from work as usual. The truck looked shabby parked next to Carlton's silver BMW. William was growing a beard for turkey hunting season. He smelled like sweat and his work clothes were caked with mud.

"Can't you change before you come get me?"

"I'd be late if I did that," William said.

"You're embarrassing me."

"If you don't like the way I look, start saving some money and buy your own damn car. Stop spending every cent you make on clothes."

"I have to look nice. I work in an office environment. Not that you'd know anything about that."

Harriet knew her words would gall him. They'd met at the U-Pick-It when she was in high school. He'd stopped by looking for work, and her father let him help out in the fields. William had always wanted to go to college but money was tight. When he asked her to marry him, she figured she might as well say yes. He was reasonably smart and reasonably handsome. And what if no one else asked?

When she graduated from high school, they got married on a June afternoon in the Methodist church she'd attended all her life, where every Ayres, for generations, had been baptized, married, and eventually eulogized. Her mother and Aunt Lydia decorated the church. White carnations, the cheapest of flowers, were attached in bunches to the ends of all the pews. Aunt Lydia had sewed the wedding gown herself. It was a bright too-white satin. Blinding really. Harriet knew it looked as cheap as the carnations when she walked down the aisle.

It had been seven years and William kept asking when she was going to be ready to have a baby. Harriet wanted to tell William the truth about Carlton. She wanted to live in that Hayes Barton house while Carlton climbed the ladder at the bank. She wanted to have children with Carlton and dress them exactly like him. She wanted to be a tennis mom and have ladies over for luncheons. Maybe she'd even have a maid to clean up all her messes so everything would be perfect, like a Brooks Brothers catalogue, when Carlton came home.

Harriet kept her mouth shut. In the mobile home positioned next to her parents' house, she would cook dinner while William watched basketball or football and shouted at the television. She would pour herself a large tumbler of box wine and fall asleep on the sofa. Every evening was just like the last.

Later, Harriet came to realize that sometimes life makes the decision for you. All you have to do is sit still and wait for it to happen. When it does, you have some pain for a while, and then you get used to the way things are. You're like a pinball shooting off in a new direction, finding new obstacles to bump into, new ramps to roll down, new ways to complicate your life.

Just when Harriet had decided to tell William everything, to confess her love for Carlton and her desire for a divorce, two things happened. First, Carlton announced he was engaged to a girl who lived in Hayes Barton, not one who only imagined it, and second, the bank laid Harriet off. It had nothing to do with her, the branch manager explained. The bank was streamlining things. Efficiency experts had ordained it. She was the newest hire. It wasn't personal.

Carlton said it wasn't personal either. His fiancée shared his goals. She wasn't married. She had a trust fund and a degree from Carolina. She was pretty and knew how to dress. She had great connections and could get him into the country club. She was plugged in in a way that would help him. Surely Harriet could understand this, he pleaded while she wept over the hood of the BMW. It had to be this way.

William was thrilled that they would now be able to start a family. He bought Harriet a heart locket where she'd someday be able to place a picture of their baby. Harriet said she couldn't be happier, that she believed her firing was for a reason.

The baby came less than a year later on a bleak February day. William said it might snow and sure enough on the way to the hospital, big fat snowflakes began to fall. As they waited for the delivery in a stuffy hospital room, William and Harriet watched from the window as the snow accumulated on the tops of the cars in the parking lot.

"Must be two inches now," William said, fascinated.

"Who cares?"

"I care. I want to tell our kid about the day he was born."

"You could say there was a blizzard and we almost froze to death on the way here. That we had a police escort."

"Why would I do that?"

"It makes a better story than on the day you were born there was two inches of snow in the parking lot."

"Why would I tell my son a lie?"

"What's wrong with a white lie here and there?"

* * *

As a young girl, Harriet liked to pull Papa's books from the rickety little bookshelf in the parlor. He only had a few, mostly Sherlock Holmes mysteries. The pages were brown, the color of iced tea. Sometimes they tore apart when she turned them, and sometimes their dustiness made her sneeze.

She was particularly drawn to *Heathen Mythology*, which had pictures of all the false gods and what they did and how cruel they could be. It was Papa's oldest book. A rat had eaten part of the cover, Aunt Lydia had pointed out with disgust. "You ought not even touch it." But Harriet did. She'd spent many hours one summer reading the biographies of each god and studying the pictures. Her favorite was Momus, the joker of Olympus and the god of joy. He made fun of the other gods and annoyed them so much that they made him leave Olympus. The book didn't say where Momus went or if he was sad after that. Couldn't the other gods see he was only having fun? He wasn't trying to hurt anyone.

There was also Nemesis, the goddess of Vengeance. She got people back for the things they did. She had wings and a sword and she watched you. And when the time was right she got revenge. It could be that you'd done bad things or you'd had nice things happen that you didn't deserve. Whatever it was, Nemesis set things back in order so no one could get away with anything for very long. Nemesis was bad news.

Harriet's Nemesis arrived one day in the form of the tattooed woman. Life was going well at the time. William was renovating Papa's old farmhouse so they wouldn't have to live in the trailer. Aunt Lydia and Uncle Hal had moved to a house on the outskirts of Raleigh to be closer to the cousins who all had jobs in the city. "Playing at being suburbanites," Harriet's mother had said, "but at least it frees something up for you."

Despite her reluctance, Harriet loved being a mother. She'd named the baby boy Ian. He had blond curls and big blue eyes. Everywhere she went people would comment on how beautiful he was. Once when she was at the grocery store, an old man stopped her and told her she was beautiful and so was her child. "You ought to have more," he said. No one had ever said she was beautiful before. Maybe she was only beautiful in Ian's presence. Maybe it was because she was finally happy. She'd even stopped buying the box wine.

But Nemesis was just around the corner, as Harriet discovered one afternoon not long after she and William had moved into the farmhouse. The renovation was almost done, and William had hired some friends to put a fresh coat of paint on the exterior. Harriet had chosen a pastel shade of yellow. She stood at a distance with the baby on her hip and watched the house transform from a mass of dull gray into something cheerful and bright.

The painters didn't notice her as she returned to the house. Their backs were to her and they were laughing.

"You bet he's seeing her. I saw him with her at the Backstreet Lounge. She was all over him."

"Hard to believe, man."

"It's true."

"What's she look like? Is she cute?"

"Yeah, she's pretty good looking. Got a lot – and I mean a lot – of tattoos, which is something that personally turns me off. But whatever floats your boat, man."

"And Harriet don't know?"

"Hell, no."

Nemesis' sword was poised at Harriet's neck in that moment. The debt was declared owed and due, but Harriet didn't react. She crept away and hoped the baby would stay silent. She went across the road to her mother's house and watched *Dr. Phil* until the painters left.

Over the next few days she began following William in the used minivan they'd bought when the baby was born. Not too close so he wouldn't notice, but close enough to keep up. Ian rode in the car seat in the back. Mostly he slept but sometimes he got hungry and cried.

"No time to eat now, sweetie," Harriet would say. "We've got to catch Daddy red-handed."

It took a few days of tracking, but she finally spotted William and the tattooed woman at a Dairy Queen. Harriet watched from the parking lot as they walked inside and sat down in a window booth. The tattooed woman had jet-black hair and bangs. She was wearing a blue vintage halter dress with a full circle skirt. And the painter was right – she had a lot of tattoos. Her back, arms, and legs were a jungle of flowers and vines, bright red, yellow, and green.

Harriet sat stunned in the minivan as the baby cried. If she'd regained her composure and left, William wouldn't have seen her. Before she could drive off, he turned his head to look out the window. They locked eyes. She started the minivan and tore out of the parking lot. All she could think about was a glass of wine. Something to calm her nerves so she could think straight again. Ian's screams were piercing. She couldn't complete a thought. Her mind was racing.

It seemed natural to pull up to the gas station and hop out for a second. She was coming right back. All she needed was a bottle of cheap wine. Something to take the edge off. She didn't think twice about it. She left Ian in the car.

She grabbed a wine bottle from the cooler and her cell phone rang. It was William. She didn't answer. She ran into the restroom and sobbed in a stall for forty-five minutes until the police came. They arrested her for child neglect. Ian was in the arms of a police officer when they led her out of the store. He was screaming, his face red and contorted, his chubby arms reaching for her as she ducked inside the police car.

* * *

The Trinket Man left that afternoon in a huff. As usual, Harriet had ordered nothing but magnets and mugs and the like. He didn't say goodbye. She glanced at her watch again. Ian would be standing at his locker with his backpack about this time. If she left now, she might be able to get a glimpse of him before Erica picked him up. She wondered if the other kids made fun of him because of Erica's tattoos or whether second graders thought that kind of thing was cool these days.

Without giving it another thought, she climbed into the minivan. All she wanted to do was set eyes on him. She didn't see him enough. Visitation was supervised. What she wouldn't give for a quiet evening alone with him. Reading together, watching television, eating popcorn, telling jokes.

She parked the minivan up the street from the school. She could already see him in the distance, waiting with the other kids beside the carpool lane. He still had the blond curls that made him easy to spot. He saw her too. It seemed normal to beckon him with an emphatic wave. It was innate. A mother had to be with her child. He ran toward her before the teachers even noticed, before Erica could exit her car and scream, "Don't let her leave with him. She doesn't have custody."

Harriet took Ian by the hand. They ran together, and, panting and out of breath, both laughing, they took off in the minivan to the farmhouse.

"Are we running away?" Ian asked, gasping. "I have a soccer game tomorrow so I'm not sure that's a good idea."

"No, just a visit to my house. It's where you lived when you were a baby."

"Okay. You got any video games?"

"How about we play the Game of Life?"

"I tried that before. It's kind of hard."

"It is hard but I'll teach you."

As the afternoon sun settled over the tree line, Harriet set up the game on the kitchen table. The board was tattered and old, and many of the tiny pink and blue pegs – the children, the husbands, the wives – were missing. Ian chose a blue car and raced it down the path of Life. Harriet told him that's not how you play but he didn't listen. She smiled and watched as he zoomed over the board, following the path at first, then diverting from it and meandering about. Harriet knew that in a little while police lights would brighten the darkening sky, flashing blue and red in the field like flames, and winged Nemesis would descend once more to enforce the inflexible rules by which life must be played.

David Dixon

Cassandra

she whispers of the casualty count
yet I am stony
          earless

for it is her curse
not mine
to disbelieve

this madwoman holding fate
          like a table for two

knowing how I sit

and welcome
inside once impervious gates

          you

like a wooden horse

Porter Huddleston

Beautiful Girl Ugly World

Once there was a young woman whose life was hard the whole way through and ended badly. She always thought it would get better, but it didn't. She was beautiful, but the world around her was not. Her youth was the fallout of a rural upbringing in Arkansas, where trash burned in rusted iron barrels on every patch of land and these served as streetlights.

In good times, shotgun butts were smashed against windshields to handle strife. In bad times, the other end held forth. In the darkest times, animals that could neither climb nor fly found themselves mysteriously transported up, over and down into neighboring wells where they died and their bodies swelled and ruptured and bled and stank and poisoned the water, and so the families drank cream and goat milk, and spooned cornbread out of plastic mugs soaked in buttermilk. Life beyond that was a fairy tale.

When her husband plucked her from the secretarial pool at 18, they struck out for a hopeful new life in Little Rock. There were neat houses with square little yards and barbecues and holidays and community events. But where most people conducted and counted themselves better, her life went differently. It was baffling. Her husband snuck through the window late at night when he was done drinking and gambling and she had locked the door and jammed a chair under the knob, and he would get caught in the blinds and curse and they would scream and fight and knock over the furniture. But there weren't guns or wells filled with dead things.

She thought she loved another man once when her sons were little, but all she got for her trouble was a go in the state hospital, either because of unrequited love or something darker she wanted to confess but couldn't. They tried shocking her back to good health to show her life was worth living, but somehow it didn't work. Things just never panned out for her.

Eventually, the world moved on and so did the woman. She and her husband arrived in the deep south with their three boys years later. Middle-aged, she learned slowly through trial and error that Atlanta was a different kind of south. She tried to fit in, which only worked out if one squinted and the light was just right. She couldn't pronounce the entrées, or the word *entrée*, when she dined downtown with her husband and his team for sales meetings. She moved through the crowd sucking in her cheeks to appear refined, but the ruse fell apart when she ordered. Steak became *fillit mignone* and the gourmet burger named for the interstate loop that circled the city became *perry meeter*.

She learned to inscribe her full name, rather than B.H., when signing in at the Atlanta Lawn and Tennis club because her initials left her name open to interpretation by the members of ALTA. At some point in her descent into suburbia, she thought her good neighbors, her husband's secretary, his sales associates or their wives were calling the house and hanging up. She would answer and there was someone on the line, but they said nothing. Other times, it was just a woman laughing. On other occasions, a gentleman would ask for someone who didn't live there. Sometimes she thought she recognized the voices; other times, she wasn't sure. She kept stacks of yellow legal pads filled with the dates, times and circumstances of each call piled next to her bed. She was sure she would cipher it out in time, but she never did.

When her sons left for college, whatever haunted her grew bolder in its malice. She feared someone or something wanted not just to toy with her, but somehow cross the barrier between the seen and unseen worlds and punish her. Security became her chief concern. All the windows in her home were nailed shut. She installed keyed deadbolt locks on every door, including her bedroom, to ward off burglars. But somehow the backdoor worked itself open in eerie defiance just the same and waited for her discovery each day. Motion detectors were added outside her bedroom, but never detected anyone.

By the time her sons left the house for good, her survival skills were worn out and her looks faded. They had packed up and left years ago with her good judgment and social skills leading the exodus. The last vestiges of the woman disembarked from her person separately, each embodying a form of her, and together boarded a MARTA train downtown and that was the last anyone saw of her. She died slowly, suffocating as her oxygen tank failed.

Finally, when she was laid to rest on the grounds where she'd lived with her husband, her yard was measured and found to be larger and better maintained than her place in people's hearts. Each foot she sunk into the ground brought a palpable sense of release in those assembled, until she reached the bottom and there was a collective sigh that said six feet deep and not deep enough.

She died in the spring as she had hoped. It was the prettiest season, and she felt it might inspire others to remember her well, which it didn't. There was some debate at her funeral about how low was low enough to bury the possibility of a haunting after the holidays, as no one put it past her, and maybe using a water well as a blueprint made the most sense, and lacking that then only the strongest possible enclosure should be used to contain her. A fat marble slab on top would help. There was no eulogy so that she didn't have time to change her mind. And the mock one that wound its way through the crowd instead was, "She lived, she died — and hopefully that's it." Except for the wailing trotted out by her husband, the congregants agreed that mourning should be rationed for a better opportunity. And so it was by most.

But not all.

Deborah Phelps

Prison Teaching

One essay styled the seven shots
The man took as an imitation of Christ,
The bullets still hot in his body.
But those essays of gore soon turned to tedium.
I wanted to know what these men had really done
To deserve this place. Child-rape? Knifed
Girlfriends? All that sick rhetoric I assigned
Each week tried to pry it out of them. No deal.
I treated them like writers. I was fair, attentive.
I encouraged and praised. I am certain
I changed not one life. Shone not one light
Elsewhere for them. Eventually, they all
Wrote me into the fairy tale: Towered princess,
Frozen, sleeping, apple-dead. Awaiting their kiss,
My resurrection. A red ribbon around my neck.

Lian Reese

Bleeding yellow

A man wanders lonesome through the night
And at each dwelling looks
To see the living done so well
By those who fear could not carry
And wanders still to other frames
To gaze at fitful sleep
As it opens all the windows
All the doors.
It is here he weary enters
But long for sleep as he might
He wanders still room to room
Weeping, sobbing, broken man
Until to this hall he wanders
Seeks, and finds,
An old man all in blue.
Breathing light and eyes half closed
His living days are through.
See how the lonesome lies with him
Seeking comfort still
And finding it in one last breath
That the dead man drew.

Anthony Howcroft

The Flavors of Savannah

Nostalgia was not our best-selling option. We would have stopped selling it years ago, but there was a niche that reliably came back for more. That was before the *Bad Times*. After that, it seemed we couldn't get enough. Nostalgia was the zeitgeist, and it didn't have the hard come-down of the high pleasure alternatives. The price rocketed, and raw materials got harder to source each week. Every guapo on the grid was mixing and selling, and we needed a way to differentiate. I told Savannah to focus her planet-sized brain on the issue.

"Why's it my problem?" she said.

"Our problem, but your specialization. You know me – distribution, planning, ops. You handle product."

She made a sound that could have been an acknowledgement, or perhaps an indication that I was a total idiot and took a sip from her frozen sunset. I was on the juice.

"Besides, I can't take any more tofein," I said. "Tofein soup, grilled tofein and watercress, tofein quesadillas. I'm sick of it." The texture was driving me crazy. I couldn't complain about the taste, because it didn't have any. "I need meat. We gotta get some denaro flowin' again."

Night-shift deep in the levels. It was slippery-hot, and I was desperate to move, but Savannah was knotted into my arms with one leg thrown across me, fast asleep. Every forty minutes the gas-turbine one zone across would fire up like a jet engine, straining to pump out the nitro-oxides, sulphur, and CO_2, the nox, sox and cox as Savvie called them. She groaned in her sleep, and I shifted position to try and find a cool patch on our thin sliver of bed. Heaven and hell, it was both. Her scent drifted up to me, and she whispered,

"I can give them what they want."

"Who?"

"Everyone," she said, then sighed, and fell back to sleep.

How she dreamt up the flavors, I don't know, but they were her masterstroke, chemo-neuro-magic. Savannah's a genius but stays in the shadows. Dresses scraggy to hold the guys away and keeps her distance from the geeks, too. Savannah and me are tight. Got her out of a few holes when it all went bad, up there. Nabbed a crib in the levels when the exodus began. Nothing fancy, but better than those communal halls, with lice in the beds and broth.

You know, real nostalgia is a positive set of memories, polished by retelling, that conveniently ignores any nasty stuff. It combines with your understanding that things turned sour later, to give that sweet taste with a bitter hint. Like remembering that post high-school vacation with your crew. You recall it as everyone being carefree, filled with laughter and romance. The memory's pure and true, if you forget about the angst and hangovers. The bad part comes because you know what followed – the girl killed by a drunken bigot in a truck, the fluke Lisfranc injury that ended your best friend's sporting career, the drudgery of real jobs, all the dreams that died. That's where the nostalgia kicks-in.

What Savannah did though, was to make our Nostalgia more than a vanilla-sensation. She figured out how to tune it for vacations, love, sporting victories, winter, childhood. She found a way to kick in the right neural transmitters to trigger specific feelings. She called them flavors. They worked differently for each person, but they were much more targeted, and repeatable. We'd hit gold but it wasn't enough for Savannah.

My shop's pretty deep in the levels, as you'd expect. No sunlight, our vit-D all comes from supplements. There's no room to swing a cat, and if I had something that valuable I wouldn't be whirring it around like an AC-fan. I have a sliding door of steel but when I'm here I leave it open and use a beaded curtain that rattles when a customer arrives. I'm normally reading, thrillers and stuff. Books are the most powerful drugs. I thank the stars they're not rationed yet. My shelves are stacked with jars that hold tablets, gels, and capsules of every shape and color. I have no idea what most of them do. I picked them up as a job-lot. Occasionally, someone finds something they want, and I try to guess what they can afford, and we haggle. Most people don't come here for the pills though, they're to make us seem legit. People want real medicine; the stuff Savannah makes.

"I'm a chemist, not a criminal," Savannah says.

"You're an artist," I tell her.

"You're full of shit," she says, but I can tell she's flattered.

The problem with the flavors was that we needed ingredients you can only get from sub-surface level, where the fat-cats and politico's live. Getting into their zone was easy, because there were good reasons for nobodies to come through the gatehouse – fixing pipes, delivering food, repairing generators, whatever. The gatehouse didn't care either, it was only a job, and they were as depressed as the rest of us. Savannah and I knew how to get past them. That's not to say we weren't nervous, the first time. I was dripping with sweat even in the air-conditioned halls of that upper zone. I was shocked at how wide the connecting spaces were. The lanes, tunnels, and even the corridors, all felt like goddam freeways. You could have squeezed two Level-29 markets down the middle of the main thoroughfare, which was decorated with brightly colored succulents.

Savannah stopped and nudged me. I followed her gaze to a tree, branches spread like arms, older than time, a real tree. They must have moved it sub-surface and built a crystal dome over its crown, where it poked above ground level. I had a flashback to a childhood picnic under the shade of an oak-tree, rubbing the red-gingham table-cloth between my finger and thumb, the texture of summer. I wanted to dwell in that memory, forever.

"Snap out of it," Savvie said under her breath.

We had checked the bootleg blueprints to plan this excursion, but it's one thing having a map in your head, and quite another following it with sunlight and a goddam tree filling your head with locked-away memories.

"This is it," Savannah said, pointing at the inspection hatch. She inserted the crypto-key and twisted.

"Over to you," she said with a tone that told me not to mess up, after the produce we'd traded for that cybertech.

I'd memorized the code. Twenty digits long. We'd probably get three attempts, but I didn't want a yellow light flashing on the gatehouse dashboard. There was a beep, a green flicker, and the center coil of the hatch popped out to reveal the handle. Savvie was smiling like a kid. I pulled the handle, and the ladder slid down.

"Ladies first," I said.

When we emerged into the residence grounds, my nerves were on fire. Everything was calm, but this was unknown territory. Theoretically, there was nobody onsite. That was the intel. Didn't mean they didn't have private security, laser-trips, thermals, drones, or another defense system. We weren't exactly experts, although it wasn't our first time at the rodeo, either.

There were panels across the surface-level ceiling, thick reinforced-acrylic, separated by joists, that made the roof a chessboard of white squares thirty foot above us. I hadn't seen this much natural light in years. The living quarters were four hundred yards away, and the grounds were like a country garden. I saw grass – real not astro – and manicured hedges. There was an orchard, densely packed with apples and pears, plus a pond with Koi carp. Damn, do these people know what it's like below? Have they seen the malnutrition, eczema, asthma, the grind for survival? They have friggin' ornamental fish basking in natural sunlight. I shook with anger.

"You know what we're here for," Savvie said. "Nothing more, let's go."

Savannah had a list of herbs for us to gather. She'd given me a chart of the simpler ones that weren't in the patch she was raiding; chewable fiber from specific roots, dock leaves, Thai-Basil, a smorgasbord of weird stuff to identify. I was on security too, keeping an eye on anything that moved, which wasn't us. Who says men can't multi-task?

I thought I might look for the items around the orchard, and maybe gather a windfall or two. I was thinking apple, but then I saw it, like a perfect setting sun in miniature; an orange. The tree was festooned. Unable to resist the temptation, I pulled and twisted one, and the branch sprang up with a rustle of leaves. The scent was to die for.

"What the hell are you playing at?"

I nearly decked Savannah, who had crept up on me. "You're making more noise than a turbine at full rotation."

I tossed her a couple of segments. "Taste that," I said.

She was about to give me some grief, but saw the juice dripping off my fingers and the aroma was overwhelming. She popped a slice in her mouth, face like murder, and bit down. Her eyes lit up, then half closed. Savannah's mouth stopped chewing, as she savored it. When her eyes opened again, they were bright and she smiled, as a bead of juice dribbled over her lip, before she wiped it and giggled. I've loved her since we were fourteen. These days, I sometimes forget, who we are, who we were.

"Take three," she said.

"I can carry more."

"One each, one to trade. Any more is trouble," she stated.

Reluctantly, I did as I was told. Well, three or six, it's pretty much the same thing. Never was much good at math.

Every excursion was an adrenalin kick. We never took too much that it would be noticed. We didn't take chances, until the seventh trip – which must have been twenty cycles after the first excursion. Savannah had found a new place to raid, with some different items she wanted.

"I'm going to call this flavor Taglia," she said.

"Like, *cut*?" I asked.

"It's a play on the last six letters of Nostalgia, and it means cut in Italian. You can also translate it as a reward, but I was thinking more of your clothing size, cut of the cloth."

"A reward, like a price on your head? What does it do?" I said.

Savannah looked wistful, "Remember that tee-shirt I had with the fox?"

I thought for a moment, "Yeh, like a collage, from tattered red and orange cloth? You wore it to death."

"I looovvveeed that shirt. When I see an old image of myself wearing that, I yearn for it, even though I'd forgotten it existed. That's the Taglia sensation."

"A desire for old clothes?" I laughed.

She kidney punched me. "The memory of things you loved, that you've now lost, dopehead."

We followed the same time, same route, same process. You might say a repeatable pattern is poor strategy. We saw it as a winning formula and since it was working, why change? Anyhow, it was the bird that started the problem, and the fact that we were ten minutes late – a diversion around a security patrol that we didn't fancy encountering. Finally, we were inside. Savannah sent me off to these rows of corn, nearly shoulder high. She wanted a dandelion, thought there might be some in the weeds, since the area looked wild. The corn rows were eighty yards long, and ten rows wide. I didn't need a chart for a dandelion, I knew exactly what the yellow lion-heads looked like. A lifetime ago, I picked one and stuck it behind Savvie's ear. Thought she would knock it out, but she gave me a peck on the cheek instead. First kiss.

I saw a movement and froze, pulled back from my memory into the job. Nothing. I edged forwards, and then the blurred movement and shrieking alarm happened at once. My brain was overloaded. It's a good thing we never carry weapons, because I'd have started shooting. Then I realized it was a bird.

Savannah arrived.

"What…" was all she said, before the alarm repeated.

"Pheasant," I said.

"Shut it up, before the whole neighborhood arrives."

There were gaps in the corn, every fifteen yards. I slipped quietly through one to find the bird. No movement. I waited and fantasized about no tofein for a few days. Pheasant breast, tender, lean meat. Pheasant stew, dripping with delicious taste. My mouth began to salivate. I saw a head jerk, a gold and black eye staring at me out of blood red feathers.

"Supper time…" I murmured enticingly, "…coo-coo-coo."

It tilted the dazzling blue and red head, as I edged closer. Suddenly, deciding I was a threat, it shot away, racing to slip through the corn. I dived forwards, but it was faster. It squawked the alarm, and this time, there was an answer. A second bird nudged out of the corn right beside me. I grabbed one wing as it darted to escape. There was a blur of feathers, claws, and a beak that I swear had teeth, plus a raucous sound like a dozen burglar alarms going wild after a storm. Savannah was back. She was ready to tear me a new a-hole, but when she saw the blood from my scratched face, feathers and shit all over me, she started laughing instead. I managed to wring the bird's neck. Brutal, but food is food.

"We'd better exit. Pronto?" I said.

Savvie was laughing so hard she couldn't respond, bent over with her hands on her knees. Then we were lit up. A bold orange spotlight like we'd walked on stage. Savannah dropped and rolled through the corn into the next row. Disorientated, I followed suit.

The spotlight was still on us, and I nearly tripped over another pheasant.

"Wait!" she said, pointing above my head.

I raised my eyes, not sure what to expect – but certainly something weaponized. I had to use my free hand to shield my eyes. The acrylic roof was blazing. Hovering in the sky was a giant orange ball of fire.

"The sun," Savvie said. It had been so long since we'd seen it.

My muscles relaxed. I felt giddy with relief. "Feel that heat," I said.

Savvie leaned forward and kissed me, full on the lips.

"One day, we should come back here when we don't have to rush…" she said, her fingers brushing under my chin.

Maybe we lingered too long. We were already running late. We'd got into the habit of locking the access tunnel behind us, so we didn't leave any rabbit-holes for the curious to follow. Then we simply unlocked again to leave. I tapped the code out twice, perfectly. The panel glowed red.

"What's the problem?" Savvie asked.

"The code has timed out," I said.

"Try it again," she said.

I shook my head. "Two fails already. Third one will trigger an alert. Let's move to Plan B."

"Do we have one?"

"That's your domain," I said.

"Shit." She looked around and started walking towards the residence. I knew there was nobody at home, or they'd have been out already thanks to the noise.

"Can't go through, but there might be a side access. Let's try there," she pointed.

We found what we needed, a steel gate with a surprisingly old-fashioned padlock.

"If I had the clippers, I could slice that off in a flash," I told her.

"If I was carrying, I could blow it away, but we don't have either," she said.

I looked around. Nothing. Popping on my LED, I peered inside the lock mechanism. It was pretty simple. If I had something narrow and hard, I might be able to tumble it. I looked at the bird swinging in my other hand.

"Hold this," I told Savvie and gave her the LED, positioning her hand so it was over the lock at the right angle. Then I switched my grip on the bird, to hold it by the claw instead of the neck. Halting the pendulum-swing of its body with my other hand I pushed one talon into the lock.

"You've got to be kidding. Picking a lock with a pheasant?" Savvie shook her head but kept the LED perfectly still.

It was clumsy, but good enough. I heard the click, tossed her the bird, and snapped the lock open. The lane was clear, as far as I could see.

"This one's going down as legend," Savannah said, silently closing the gate. We walked calmly towards the gatehouse. There was a gentle breeze, which should have acted as a warning.

"STOP!" a digitized-voice yelled.

We turned, a security drone gliding towards us, all carbon-fiber gun-barrels and whirring blades.

"Go," Savvie mouthed to me, and she spun like a discuss-thrower, to hurl the throttled bird into the low-flying drone. It was a direct hit, from both parties. The drone veered sideways to smash into the curved wall, rotors and feathers scraping down the metal, as Savvie crumpled to the floor. A rose-red stain flowering across her chest.

"Go," she whispered again, and her eyes closed for the last time.

You know the rest. I didn't leave her, but I got a lenient sentence, all things considered. The shop keeps me going. I've got enough stock for a few more months. After that, who knows? Life's hard, but that's nothing new. I replayed those excursions in my head, in my cell, and now when it's quiet here. The drops of fresh orange spilling over her lips, Savvie doubled over laughing, the sunlight giving her a halo, as it caressed our skin with its warm, once familiar touch. Then again, I'm using. Catch me un-flavored and I might tell you Savannah was selfish, with no back-up plan. That she never really loved me. I was a tool to get her ingredients. She was a messy eater. We overheated under the radioactive ball of gas that pollutes our wasted planet. As the sun fried our brains, we made mistakes. Neither of us saw the alarm wire on the doorframe. A single point four-zero caliber round fired at close range from a DRJ-Kestrel drone, that left an exit wound bigger than a crater. Just another petty criminal snuffed out by our efficient law enforcement teams.

That's not how I see it, though, even when I'm off-cycle. I kept the dwindling stocks of pure Nostalgia for myself, at first. But in these dark days, we could all use a little more light, and I started giving it out for free, to the customer's I liked – the one's with respect, the people that kept some humility even in this hellhole.

Savvie never got to make the Taglia flavor – enhancing the memory of things you loved, that you lost. Not sure I need it. My memories are sweet and sharp enough. She got the name right, though. It cuts like a damned knife.

Mark Caskie

Cairns

1
In Scotland,
I found them in fog, and deeper
into a cloud band they led.
Old lichen covered piles
all shaggy bearded, squatting
prehistoric men turn to
cold, mute stone. I
stumbled on sheared shards,
and though I watched
not once did they breathe. Those
dark silhouettes on the hillside.

2
You reached the top first, and when
I caught up
I found the stones in your hands.
The pile was as big as a car.
Hikers milled about drinking water
eating gorp,
their bright jackets and packs
hurt my eyes.
I added my rocks as well,
some had been spray-painted.
I thought of hands against stone,
how we all come to hate scree.

3
The magazine shows
them like giants,
signposts for Inuits,
bleak and treeless land.

4
If Gary Snyder is right, then words
are also stones.
I think of galleries full
of minerals encased in glass,
the beveled, purple interiors
of geodes,
chalky cliffsides of sulfur,
of bat-dark phosphorescence.
Dictionaries,
Poems piles together into books.

5
Back in the Depression, the hobos would
leave small inconspicuous cairns
by roadsides, near houses where meals
could be had. My grandmother
made them stand on the porch,
eating cold chicken or a bowl of soup.
They always returned the plate,
inquired about work thereabouts.
In their eyes, the freights ran.
In their clothes, the alley smell of cities.
Cairns no higher than shoe tops
guided them from meal to meal.

Claire Thomas

Trash Island

I was relieved that I hadn't packed my customary bottle of gas station Prosecco when the police officer approached me on the beach. Various books were placed in the corners of my blanket to keep their edges down against the wind as he treaded through the sand. "Excuse me, miss. Have you seen a woman's boot? It's black" he asked once I was in earshot. I told him I had stepped over one as I walked towards the waterline and that I remembered it being close to the makeshift fire pit made out of old tires. He thanked me and proceeded to study the area. Five minutes had passed when he returned to my blanket. "You may want to find another spot. This is believed to be a crime scene and the sheriff's department will be here soon. Don't want your car blocked in".

This took place at Fiesta Island and this is the story I often use to describe it. Known between my friends and I as "Trash Island", it is a 485 acre plot of land within the entanglement of San Diego's Mission Bay. It's a place locals can visit to shamelessly flick cigarette butts and swim in their jeans. Cowboy hat-wearing men rev their jet skis towards shore partnered with topless women and ask if you want a turn. It is also said that the island is secretly a mass burial site for discarded whales, with the adjacent lot being home to Sea World.

After the crime scene incident, I began spending my time on the island's north shore. To get there, I would park my car next to a sand bank where the paved road began to curve. I walked to where the dunes sat high off the road, watching for broken beer bottles and miscellaneous scrap. Gracelessly, I would slide down the dunes to a narrow beach hidden from the road and all fellow island dwellers. I went most Saturdays, some Sundays and the occasional Tuesday if I was able to leave work early. I would often stick a branch into the sand and dangle the plastic bag containing a cheap bottle of wine into the bay water to keep it chilled. From my blanket, I would watch interstate traffic from across the water and the drooping palm trees lining distant neighborhood streets.

I had cried there. I had received great news and I had received terrible news there. I had fallen in love with book passages and song lyrics there. I had even burned the wooden pallets once used as my bedframe there. From three thousand miles away, I still go to the island, if only in my mind. I think of the particular smell of nearby trash fires and the sound of lapping water after a boat had passed and I wonder: did that woman ever get her boot back?

Janet Joyner

Risky Business

It's not as though
there were no signs,
no melting glaciers,
or dead whales washing
up on our shores; no
spiraling loss of species,
nor the warming winters.
Suddenly, a terrible
connectedness.
With dead bodies
piling up
curbside.
And against
Stuyvesant's wall.

Joyce Schmid

After a Storm

Our pink azalea bursts in blossom,
every inch of it. The plum tree
did the same last year, erupting
in red-purple fruit. Then poof!
It died.

Is too much joy unstable,
or a danger sign?

Well, sign me up.
Allow me just a day in bloom,
no twisted branch left bare,
leaf-buds humming in the meristem,
impatient to be born.

Anthony Howcroft

Laughing at Funerals

The boss told us it was an easy job, but there's no such thing. We weren't born yesterday. It isn't a full removal though, only a piano. We've shifted plenty before and they're bloody heavy, and tricky too, because you can't dismantle them. At least this time there's no owner hanging around, screeching like a minah bird at the first sign of danger. I don't like having to deal with customers, I prefer my dealings to be solid and trustworthy. An old coffer, a dresser, book cases, chairs and tables – they all do what they're meant to and live much longer than us, serenely shifting owners with barely a murmur. Pianos are an exception, a necessary evil. This instrument looks ancient. The thing weighs a ton because it's made of real wood, not those thin planks they bang together for modern instruments. I tickle a few notes, and the boss tells me to stop messing about and get a dust sheet. I'd say the keys are real ivory. We load her up and hop in the van. Andy's driving, Neil's the navigator, while the boss and I squeeze into the middle of the van's bench seat.

"Head towards Margate," Neil says.

I suck in my breath. "Enemy territory," I say.

"Brace yourself," the boss runs a hand over his balding head. "We'll be deep in Yorkshire. Better stay silent, don't want anyone t'catch tha' Blackpool accent."

I tell them, "My grandfather was a passionate Lancastrian. Red rose to the bone."

"Wasn't he a tradesman?" the boss asks.

"Yeah, a sparky. We always knew when the Electric Board were coming. He'd rig the meter to run backwards for a few days. I remember hiding behind the sofa with my mam while the officials hammered on the door."

The boss laughs, "Cheeky blighter!"

"He was a black sheep, but fun. Could make the devil laugh, that one. Caught up with my grandfather in the end. Too many ciggies, too many bars. Cancer."

The other three nod, we've all lost someone that way.

"He stayed with my mam's twin when he got bad. She's in Howarth. He didn't live much longer. I went to the funeral. We had one of those big black cars to follow the hearse, for the family. As we drove along my Uncle suddenly turned and told me, *your grandfather always said he wouldn't be seen dead in Yorkshire*."

Neil and Andy guffaw.

"It's true as well, my grandfather used to say those exact words. Anyway, we pull up outside the crematorium and can't stop laughing. There's the rest of the family and his friends, all waiting outside, nearest and dearest. We're staggering out of the car with tears of laughter streaming down our faces. Should've seen their looks. Nothing we could do though, it's a family curse, we always laugh at funerals."

Neil glances at the map. "You should have taken that left," he says.

Andy gives him a look, "Shall I turn?" he asks.

The road's very narrow, with a stone wall on one side and a ditch on the other. Any three-point turn is going to be tricky.

"No," Neil says, turning the map on its side. "Take the next left. I mean right."

Andy shakes his head and sighs. He slows down and keeps a look out for the next right. The boss peers out of the window, deep in thought.

"Can't afford to get lost today, lads," the boss finally says. "I want to be settled in by the goggle-box with a cold Guinness, long before kick-off."

By one o'clock, we're lost. Neil tilts the map carefully as though it's one of those parlour games where you navigate a silver ball through a maze. We're looking for an isolated rural house nestled between the canal and railway. We have a photo. It feels like we're close, but there don't seem to be enough bridges. Twice, we've followed a road that parallels the railway, and then curls away to a bridge, where we loop over and find ourselves trapped by the canal.

"What next?" Andy asks.

"Does this look familiar?" Neil answers.

"Give me the damned map," the boss says.

I stare across the railway at the fields. There's a smattering of trees, an old water trough, and a house that looks a thousand years old.

"Wait!" I yell.

Andy slams on the brakes, and the back of the truck zings like a startled xylophone.

"Isn't that it?" I point to the house across the railway line.

The boss gets the photo off the dashboard. "Good man," he slaps me, playfully.

Andy pulls over. We climb out of the cabin and stretch. The house is less than fifty yards away. Unfortunately, the railway line is between us, with a steep embankment either side, as the track is thirty feet below the road's level. Andy shakes his head.

"We need a bridge," he says.

The boss glances at his watch. "We've tried that. We'll take it down and across," he says authoritatively.

Neil looks down the line, which curves so you can't see more than a quarter mile from our vantage point. "What if a train comes?"

The boss considers that. "It's probably disused. They've shut down most of these regional lines."

We all stare at the track. It doesn't look disused. There are no weeds pushing up the sleepers and the rails look polished.

The boss reads our minds. "There'll be one train an hour, worst case." Nobody moves. "Well, what are you waiting for?" He asks. "It's a fixed-price contract, you're not getting paid by the hour. Let's get lively."

Neil rigs up some ropes, while Andy and I shift the piano onto a wheelie cart. The bank looks slippery. I grip the dust sheet, more for balance than any pretence I could hold it if the ropes let out too fast. Andy's on the other side, doing the same. Neil and the boss puff as they lower it, a handful of rope at a time.

"What other funerals have you laughed at, then?" Andy asks.

"My aunt's. We're singing some hymn I've never heard. It's like guess the tune."

"Then stay silent," Andy says.

"That's exactly what I decide for the second hymn, but I mouth along so nobody can tell. I glance left, and my brother's doing the same, the two of us opening and shutting our mouths like bloody goldfish."

"That would set me off," Andy says.

"We fell apart. My stomach heaving, trying not to laugh aloud. The hardest part's after the song finishes, and we have to sit quietly through the serious parts."

"Agony," he says.

"People think the whole family's heartless because we laugh when we should cry. Doesn't mean we're crazy, right?"

"Unless you cry when you should laugh," Andy says.

The piano lurches forward. "Woah, steady!" Andy calls.

I look left for a train. Nothing. I'm sweating buckets.

Soon, the piano rests at the bottom of the embankment. Now we need to haul it on to the other side. Neil takes the rope up the opposite bank to find something to hook it around. We watch him scrabble and slide. His feet scrape away grass to leave dark channels of mud. His knees and hands are brown when he turns around at the top.

"The rope won't stretch to the house, and there are no trees," he says.

"Let's try brute force," the boss says. He sends me to join Neil, leaving himself and Andy to push from below. They lean their backs into the piano. I'm standing behind Neil at the top of the embankment, like we're in a tug-o-war competition.

"Go!" shouts the boss.

The rope moves with surprising ease at first, and I take two paces back. Neil is straining in front of me, and my feet slide as I try to get more grip. With another xylophone-like sigh from the piano, Neil and I are dragged back to our starting position. The boss commands us to try again, with more effort, but the result is the same.

"Is this the Chorley line?" Andy asks.

He gets a mouthful from the boss. Neil and I laugh, but we're not the ones standing on the track. The boss sends me to the house to see if the owner has a car for a tow. His instructions include some direct consequences regarding my future ability to father children, if I don't act quickly. I sprint to the building, vault over a wall, and look for signs of life. The place looks closed. There are no cars in the driveway, although there are plenty of outhouses where you could store a vehicle. I bang three times on the door with my fist. Silence. I'm about to turn back when I hear the bolts being thrown open. The door swings and an older man stands there with a mop of silver hair, although he still has a slim and athletic build.

"Let me guess," he says, holding up a finger. He cocks his head to one side and says, "You've come about the piano, haven't you Paul?"

"Do I know you?" I ask.

"I know your grandfather. Fine pianist."

I should tell him that he's dead, but it's awkward, and besides, I don't have time.

"Self-taught," I say, proudly. "Never had a single lesson but can play anything."

The man smiles warmly, "I've seen him perform in bars, for drinks and tips. The life and soul…" he snaps out of his reverie. "You must think I'm terribly rude," he says, "Come inside."

"Actually, I came for help. Do you own a car with a tow hook?"

He looks at me quizzically, and I ramble. "The piano, your piano, is stuck on the railway line, sorry about that, we got into a little trouble with the navigation, and anyway, long story short, we need to pull it out. Do you have a car? Or a tractor?" I pause for a moment, not quite sure how he's going to react. As I said, I'm not so good with customers. When he doesn't respond, I add, "We have our own rope."

"That might come in handy," he says dryly, and steps inside the house, leaving the door wide open. I'm not sure if I'm meant to follow. The house is black inside, and I can't see a thing.

"Hello?" I call.

"Come in," he shouts.

I scrape my muddy feet on the mat, and step inside. There's a dim glow ahead and I follow it, groping my way down the hall, smacking my head hard on a low beam that I didn't see. It throbs, and I know I'll have a huge egg there later.

"Watch out for the beam," he calls.

I wobble into the kitchen, rubbing my head, feeling dizzy. It's hot, and there's a muscular wood-burning stove crouched in one corner. The man sits at a table where a tiny stub of candle is lit. He gestures for me to sit down, and sensing my hesitation, tells me there's only one train per day.

"Do you know what this is?" He nods at the long yellow flame.

I shake my head.

"It's an inch of candle. An auction. You place bids, and counter bids, until the candle goes out. Last bid wins. Very traditional, but out of fashion these days."

"We need to get something to pull the piano," I say, not sure what's happening.

"Precisely. I can do that, but what are you going to bid for my help?"

"It's your piano, isn't it? Don't you want it saved?" I'm confused.

"Let's say you start at a farthing. Then if you win the auction, you pay me and I help rescue the piano and your friends. Does that sound fair?"

"I don't get it," I say. "Besides, you can't have an auction with only two people."

He takes a drag on his cigarette while he looks at me. Slowly he exhales, and the smoke spirals and twists. He taps his cigarette rhythmically on an ashtray. The smoke looks fragile, like caramel or strings of treacle toffee. I imagine you could snap a tiny piece off, and the rest would collapse and shatter.

"Two's company, three's a crowd," he smiles. "I'll counter-bid the tip of your little finger." He wiggles his own fingertip but looks at mine and smiles again, then feigns concern. "Unless you play the piano - you don't though, do you Paul?"

I shake my head, "What did you say your name is?"

"The candle's burning. I'd make a bid and then ask a question, if I were you. A little hint from the wise," he brushes the smoke away.

"A penny," I say.

"For my thoughts? That's underselling, don't you think? Not to sound arrogant, but really, are anyone's contemplations that worthless?"

I'm not sure what the hell this guy's doing, but I don't like it. I've had enough of his game. I stand up, and my chair scrapes in a chalk-on-blackboard way.

"I need to get back," I tell him. A part of me expects to find my feet rooted to the ground, or the door swinging shut and locking behind me. Old houses give me the creeps. I walk clumsily towards the hall.

"Of course," he says, and I stop to listen. "The candle keeps burning, and if you're not here to bid, then my next offer wins by default. Once you've started a candle auction, you can't finish until the flame is out. Those are the rules."

I should keep walking, but I don't. There's no supernatural power holding me from the door, only fear. It's a powerful force. My head throbs, and my feet itch to run.

"How about three years' bad luck?" he offers.

"That's..." I was going to say crazy, but this whole thing is mad, and instead, the word "excessive," slips out.

"Really? I thought it was rather considerate. You get seven years for breaking a common mirror, and in your line of work that must be a frequent occurrence."

People often think that, but we're careful. Things do get broken, that's inevitable. Some of the stuff we move has rotted in place for sixty years. Certain items end up like egg shells, the slightest nudge and they collapse to dust. We always take the blame. Mirrors though, we treat with care. We're hugely superstitious. We avoid walking under ladders, crossing paths with black cats, and none of us would ever challenge the devil to a game of chess. Of course, he's smart enough to trick you into playing his games.

I walk back to the table, knock on wood, and make my next bid. "Two bob," I say. "And tell me the rules again."

"I've told you. It's simple," and for the first time I hear annoyance in his voice.

"You need to repeat them, given the stakes. Doesn't that sound fair?" I parrot his earlier words back at him.

He laughs, "Nice try. Keep me talking, eh? Let the candle burn down while your bid is on the table. It's like any other auction, Paul. Only the ending is unpredictable, a touch chaotic. Bidding starts slow, and speeds up towards the end, as people get desperate."

That's exactly what I'd realised about a minute ago. It's a sucker's game. He wins whatever happens. If we keep upping the price, before you know it I'll be waging a fortune against my soul. Even if I win, I won't be able to pay. Of course, he'll let me win. He's a con-artist, out to make money. That's what I tell myself, because I prefer that explanation to the alternative.

"Five funerals a year," he says.

"What does that mean?" I ask.

"It means you'll attend five funerals every year," he says, in a matter-of-fact way.

"Whose funerals?"

"You can't know in advance because that would spoil the fun." He stubs the cigarette out in the ashtray.

"Spoil the fun?" I say, incredulous.

"Sure. You love funerals, don't you? You're always laughing at them." His eyes scare me. Plus the fact that he seems to know a lot about my life. I reason, he must have heard me talking to Andy, a few minutes earlier. He's good at what he does, I'll give him that. "It could be family, friends, lovers, neighbours, children," he says. "Or a handful of work colleagues on a railway line. People you know well enough that you'll be obliged to attend."

"Two bob and a farthing," I tell him.

"Now that's not fair, is it?" he says, fixing his stare on me.

"Why not?" Delay, delay, delay.

I see him glance at the candle. I can't remember exactly how high it was when we started, but he'd said it was an inch. Looks like half an inch left.

"The bidding should go up with incremental stages. Sixpence, Shilling, Florin, Half a Crown, a Pound," he looks offended as he explains this.

"What happened to the full crown? You can't leap from half a crown to a pound. That's not incremental. You're bending the rules in your favour. Not that it was in the rules."

Keep talking I think, and resist the urge to glance at the candle because I don't want him doing the same. "I asked you to clarify the rules. I don't remember anything about the bidding going up in stages. You can bid anything, as long as it's an increase. If you ask me – "

"The eternal soul of your first-born child," he says, deadpan.

"Christ," I say, which might be a mistake. "Isn't that a bit clichéd?"

He shrugs. "Tradition often sounds that way. I don't normally jump ahead in the bidding, but since you're breaking our accord with your penny-pinching bids, you're giving me permission to do so as well. You see, there are unwritten rules. We'd be here all day if I had to explain those. No fighting, for example. This is a civilized auction. We should keep it that way, don't you think?"

I nod assent.

"I'm glad you agree." He launches into a monologue about the state of society and the value of manners, and I listen, drawn in by his patter and wit. I must admit he's fascinating. I'm not entirely sure what his game is, but I feel obliged to keep playing. Vaguely, I register that I haven't made another bid yet. If he is a con-artist, the best strategy would be for me to lose the auction, so I don't owe him anything. Let him win. I'm not sure I'm entirely comfortable with that approach, and I wonder if he's delusional. He's certainly mesmerising. Hypnotically, he lights another cigarette, and the smoke seems to stop and start in the air, as though there's a bubble of time which he can control at will. The smoke rolls forward and backward while his words tangle around me. Something about his gesture reminds me of my grandfather. Not sure what he did exactly that sparked that memory, if it was deliberate, or if it matters.

My grandfather was wiry-haired, with a raucous laugh. He used to smoke in the evenings, with a towering ashtray beside his chair, that would topple at the slightest nudge. I recall him sitting there, with the smell of chicken soup brewing in the pressure cooker, which was divine, and the high-pitched whistle the cooker used to make, like the sound of an approaching train. We would play cards, drink dandelion and burdock, and everybody would be laughing. Sometimes we'd sing as he played the piano. Wasn't there something important I had to do about a piano? The candle flame I'm staring at flickers. *The piano.* What could be so important about that? I let it go. I remember my grandfather's smiling face, his earthy smell as he tucked me into bed, and the coughing of an unseen lodger in the room below. Every night, my grandfather would kiss me on my forehead, turn and –

"A crown," I say, alert in the kitchen with the silver-haired man. I know what to do. I snap my arm across the table and snuff out the candle with my thumb and forefinger, like my grandfather did every night. The room goes black.

For a few moments, I daren't move. Or maybe I remain where I am for longer. I feel disorientated. My head throbs, and I rest it in my hands. The light from the stove has been extinguished, and it's bitterly cold, as though the fire has never been on. Opening my eyes, I stand and cautiously navigate my way across the kitchen, to throw open the window shutter. A welcome ray of light penetrates the darkness. I'm alone. Quickly, I head across the kitchen towards the hallway that leads outside. Then I stop, and dig deep into my pockets. I pull out half a crown, two shillings and a sixpence, and go back to leave them on the table.

"There are rules," I say aloud. Good money gone to waste, is what I think, but I recall my grandfather telling me *better to be safe than sorry.*

The hall is black. I hear a whistle, a long, slow, deep blow that changes pitch. The train is arriving. I can feel it in my feet, tonnes of steel hurtling down the line, making the ground reverberate. I rush down the corridor, almost tripping as I suddenly remember to duck beneath the beam, and then burst outside. Blinded at first by the light, it takes a moment before I can take in the scene. The smoke of the engine is pouring into the sky from the depths of the sunken embankment. It's too close and too fast. I race towards the line, shouting and screaming at everyone to run, but it's futile because I can't out-pace the train. It screams past, the whistle transforming from a peep to a howl. I stop, and as the sound retreats, I hear laughter. To my side, half hidden by the wall, stand Neil, Andy, my boss and the piano.

A rope is attached to the huge instrument, and loops through to a tractor. I feel like a total idiot. One bang on the head and I go delirious. I should retrace my steps and collect my money, but I know that's not going to happen.

"Fat good you were," yells the boss over the disappearing train. "It's a good thing this gentleman came along or the piano would be halfway to Chorley."

The silver-haired man sitting on the tractor smiles. I want to laugh, I really do.

Instead, I cry.

Bob Wickless

A Prayer for Mike, Leaving Wheeling

He rolls his chair
To the corner of the bar
And reaches out
To shake my hand.
"I'm Mike," he says.
We drink. He alternates
Using his one good arm
To swill long neck Budweisers down
And smoke countless cigarettes.
"You from Wheeling?" he finally asks.
I'm not. "Then you're
A lucky man. I've been here
Thirty-three years. That's
How old I am." I nod,
Then shake my head, and drink.
"Shit, man, in another
Five or six
I'm going to blow this place.
I don't care
What anybody thinks."
We order two more beers.

"I'm a Harley man," he says,
Although I probably could have guessed.
The Harley emblem, silver wings,
Is everywhere—
Emblazoned on the shirt
Across his chest,
On his jacket, stamped
In the silver ring he wears.
"I used to be a biker, man.
You believe that?" I do.
"Back before my wreck, that is."
I ask him of the obvious.

"Christ, no," Mike says.
"If I'd been on my bike
I wouldn't be in this chair.
I was in a *car*, man.
Smacked my head
When the son-of-a-bitch flipped.
I was just minding my own business,
Drinking a beer
In the middle of the back seat.
No one else was even hurt.
Isn't that some shit?"
Mike shakes his head, eyes
A waitress's firm breasts,
Who he good-naturedly kids,
Throws back the remainder
Of his beer.

"I was in a coma
For thirty-three weeks.
One week asleep
For every year I've wasted,
Pissed away here.
That's what I tell people
When they ask." I ask
Where he wants to go to next.
"Arizona, man. I've been drunk
With nearly everybody,
All different kinds of people
Who pass through here.
But you know what?" I don't.
"I've never been drunk
With an Indian," Mike says.
"I want to go to Arizona
So I can get drunk
With a bunch of Indians.
I never drank *firewater*, man.
You probably think I'm crazy.
You probably think

That's a hell of a thing
To want to do with your life,
Some kind of stupid-ass plan.
But let me tell you
I'm not drunk, not yet,
And I'm not crazy either, man."

Tonight, thank God, when I sleep,
Heavily, from too many long beers,
May I center my few dreams
On a brand new, fully-dressed
Harley Davidson.
May I zero in, past
The blinding chrome,
Above the big twin's V
In front of the custom seat,
To the simple Harley emblem
Emblazoned
On the teardrop-shaped tank.
And, if there may still be
Gods for poets and bikers alike,
May those stout American wings
Slowly unfurl, begin to beat,
And that huge engine crank
To pull with a hurricane's strength
Through the night sky
Above Wheeling.
And may Mike then mount
And simply ride out on his own
Once more,
To his beloved Indians
Waiting in Arizona.

Earl Carlton Huband

Looking Back at Farm Life

"I am the master of my fate" – William Ernest Henley

I. Dead Man's Curve

My mother was born into a family with lead feet. All her siblings loved fast cars. Hell, even my grandmother, even on Sunday on her way to the Gum Swamp Free Will Baptist church, drove like there was no tomorrow.

My youngest aunts were only teenagers, but rumor had it they were on a first-name basis with every highway patrolman in Pitt County. On one memorable occasion, Aunt Thelma was pulled over with Aunt Louise by her side. "Quick, switch places," said Louise. "I'll handle this one."

As the handsome young officer approached, Aunt Louise started pumping the gas pedal and racing the engine. "Lieutenant Dan," she gushed, "thank God it's you. My accelerator is sticking, and for the life of me I can't seem to make it stay unstuck."

Back then NC Highway 33, in its convoluted route around the Pitt County airport, included an especially bad S curve. Years later my sister, on my Uncle Arnold's motorcycle, took off there, watched a road sign fly by, and crash-landed in a ditch — muddy, but unbowed.

But back to my aunts. I was eleven, squeezed into the middle of the T-Bird's front seat, Louise on my left, Thelma on my right, heading into the S curve. Louise, laughing, let go of the wheel and said, "Here, you drive!"

II. Tongue Tied

When I was twelve, a city boy staying at my grandmother's Pitt County farm, my uncle Ernest finally let me drive the mule-powered tobacco truck from the field back to the stable. That wasn't hard, I thought, but then my uncle told me to unhook the mule's harness from the truck. As mules go, Old Bones was well-behaved, but even a city boy knew it was unwise to dawdle behind a mule while trying to unhook a harness.

I took too long. Old Bones started shifting his feet. His back right foot landed on top of my own right foot, scraping the skin and drawing blood. "You better clean that up quick, boy," barked my uncle. "You could get lockjaw." I hotfooted it back to the farmhouse. As I was washing my foot in the sink out back, my cousin appeared. He said, "You could get lockjaw, you know."

I nodded knowingly. I didn't know what lockjaw was, but I knew, whatever it was, I didn't want it. And I didn't want my country cousin to know that I didn't know. So that night, at bedtime, I opened my mouth as wide as I could and inserted my fingers to measure how wide open my mouth was. Morning and night, for the rest of that week, I re-measured to see how far I could open my mouth. I figured, as long as my jaw didn't start to lock up, I would be OK.

III. Learning to Talk Farm Talk

My sister, planted in a city suburb and looking to economize, hungered for a vegetable garden. Promising a cornucopia of cheap produce, she urged our mother to spring for an elaborate and expensive underground sprinkler system. Uncle Ernest, a hard-working farmer, listened closely as mother described sister's plans for her very own piece of Eden, and then he observed: "You can buy a lot of vegetables for a thousand dollars. . . ."

A friend of my Uncle Wiley was explaining to me the now-defunct tobacco allotment system: it limited each farmer to a fixed number of acres, but this friend planned to increase his acreage by renting half of my uncle's allotment. The talk turned to corn, then soybeans, then peanuts. Uncle Wiley remarked that last year "Uncle Sam" paid him so many dollars per acre for all the peanuts he didn't grow, this year he thought he might double his acreage. . . .

Like my uncles, my mother had graduated from a hard-working school of hard knocks, but I didn't think she had much of a sense of humor. Late in life I learned, to my chagrin, that she loved to tell my siblings about the time we drove past a cow standing out in a field and I observed what a big dog it was, to which my mother replied, "Son, we've got to get you back to the farm."

Kelly Jones

Castanea Dentata (American Chestnut)

my great grandfather spoke of you
in golden tones reserved only for
saviors and poets
long and strong
straight and narrow
as an appalachian preacher

your timber a bestowal from the heavens
forests, fences, furniture
in endless supply
a sign that surely god had blessed this land
of tenuous hills and reluctant soil
that lies at the feet of
ancient monuments to nature's persistence

sacred songs were sung honoring your fruitful gifts
while all across the mountains and the valleys
straight-grained men made reverent homes
from your sturdy stalks
built to shelter a world
where fire and ice take communion

but progress steamed its way across the hilled fences
on steeled tentacles that wrapped around your roots
gluttonies that coveted distant forests
carried the spores of your doom
and quicker than autumn pricks the mountain tops
you were gone- fallen like nameless soldiers
from forgotten wars
even the rugged crosses made from your limbs
were crucified for the revolution
that aspired to ordinary flatness
in a world of treeless, steeled monotones

as blessing and curses ebb and flow
progress pulps all in its way
men now build wavering homes of pine and birch
huddling worriedly in the wrathful night
praying for safety to a god
who has turned to rust
waiting for a resurrection that will never come.
mourning for the momentary saplings that
look questioningly at the sky
kneeling slowly, bending imperceptibly,
toward nothingness.

David Dixon

Invasive Species

how else can I explain the wisteria?
royal and full in the passing trees,

with its rapacious truth
that need be so extreme,

the many layers and distances
          of its spread,

twining clockwise
around any available support,

to overtake and choke
in its own hardy dispersal,

like a beautiful
and seductive poison

planted years ago with purpose
in our own backyard

Anthony Howcroft

Race for the pot

I found a lump today, while I was at work. If I slip two fingers between my shirt buttons, I can feel a swelling beneath the skin, bigger than a coin. It's firm and not particularly squidgy, although I haven't had the courage to push too hard. Everyone knows that a lump means cancer. The sooner you get it treated, they say, the higher your chance of survival. I should go to the doctor, but my philosophy has always been that it's better to live in hope than face a harsh and hostile truth. Plus, I'm scared-to-death of doctors and I've much bigger problems – the dean will kill me if I don't find him four lobsters in the next two hours.

I walk through the inner quad. Sunlight pours through the branches of the gigantic elm tree, and I pause in the cloisters and watch light spilling over its leaves in a cascade of blues. I think about my sister who is deeply religious, she would tell me to have faith. While we share a sense of humour, our world view is very different. I consider the number of times I've stopped to look at this elm tree in its various moods, branches tearing holes in the mist, or late summer rays setting the crimson leaves alight. The pagans worshipped dryads, picked omens from the arc of a swallow's flight or the rasping hoot of an owl. They grasped for meaning in nature's beauty. If I had a religion, that might be mine. I listen carefully to see what advice the elm might offer in my hour of need, but it whispers too quietly, while the diffused cobalt light swirls around me. I turn, knock on a wooden panel, and step out of this sanctuary into the narrow lane.

The gargoyles leer at me from the roof. I pass a cluster of ultra-polite Japanese tourists. They are crouching, cameras on mini-tripods with tilting heads gawking at the grotesques. For some superstitious reason, I avoid treading on their shadows, in case my bad luck is contagious.

I could have sent Andy or Steve on this shellfish errand, but the lump has made me restless. I need to meander in the hope that life may rediscover me. There's nobody in the present who I would trust with my news, who wouldn't find it a burden. I would rather stumble across a ghost from my past. With the right person, I could find deliverance. We could wander through shadowed streets and talk of the dreams we cling to, no matter how faded or tattered they seem.

The city wall curls away from me, and the honeyed stone feels rough against my palm. The sky is sharp blue, and the sunlight cuts, slicing the road as it slashes through gaps in the buildings. I walk on and realise it's too bright for ghosts. The past has gone, leaving me marooned in the here and now, with no bridge to the future.

Dinner is only a few hours away and I need to get those damned lobsters that the dean foolishly promised his guests. He never checks with us first. I think he does it deliberately, testing me, to prove my lack of value – a man of no degree.

I walk past Radcliffe Camera. The building is encircled by iron spikes that keep foreigners and locals a safe distance from the rarefied intellectuals within. Gathered outside the Camera is a group of laughing students in their late teens. They block my way, but not deliberately. They seem unaware of anyone or anything other than their tight-knit group. I vividly remember being that age; hammering out rhythms on cedar-faced guitars, picnicking on fresh figs, seeing love reflected by a pair of earth-coloured eyes, long since lost. I ponder whether my life consists of an allocated number of months, a tally of heartbeats, or if it would be better measured in memories.

Inside the Covered Market, I pass the cheese counter. I have no appetite. A young customer orders a wedge of Oxford Blue as I pass by. Hooked outside the butcher's is a hind, a brace of pheasant, and the delivery bike, high enough to stay out of reach of all but the most athletic students. A few more steps and I reach the fishmongers. In the queue, I can't resist the urge to slip a finger between my shirt buttons and circle the lump. I've been vaguely aware of it for at least a month. Sliding into bed late at night, I've sensed a fault, like that annoying rattle in the car that you only notice when a passenger makes a passing comment. The fishmongers have nothing left but ice and whitebait, plus one sad looking salmon, slit from neck-to-tail. I gesture to Billy, the owner.

"Lobster?" I say.

He shakes his head. "Four am tomorrow. You want me to hold some?"

"Nothing in the freezer?" I ask.

"Sorry, mate."

I lurk by the designer cake shop and consider my next move. Sugary brides and grooms dance on violins and parachute over cakes. There's an impressive model of Christ Church college with a crowd of marzipan guests.

"Marvellous," an Amerian lady says, admiring the confectionary.

"You know," I say, "that all food kills you?"

"Everything kills you in excess," she replies, tapping her fingernails on the window.

"Food is a murderer, even in moderation. We're like cars. You have to use fuel to power the car, but the little impurities and particles eventually clog the engine."

"Like salt?"

"One day salt is the killer, and red wine is healthy. The next day they switch roles, because all food types have a lethal capacity as well as a benefit."

"Salt is always bad," she says.

"So why do they use saline drips at the hospital?" I ask. She concedes the point and I continue. "You need food, but it blocks the arteries, fills the brain with heavy metals, thins the skin, and wears you down."

The woman is wearing a white dress with a subtle blue pattern that reminds me of the scattered light from the elm tree.

"How do you know all this?"

"I'm a chef," I say.

"Ahhh," she smiles. "Then what *should* I eat?"

"Anything you want. We all die so you might as well enjoy yourself."

"Fascinating. I'm no expert, but I have found that sometimes your theory is reversed – food can save your life. A pleasure to meet you."

She holds my hand tightly, not releasing it until she has finished, marking the end of our dialogue. Staring at her reflection in the shop window as she walks away, I see the candy college and I know where to try next, Christ Church. They're sure to have a few lobsters, and the master-chef is a good guy. As I rush out of the Covered Market, I pass the jewellers, where every watch seems to be counting down time, just for me.

The porter at the college doesn't recognise me, so I flash my ID, but he's busy with a group of Spanish teachers and their unruly mob. Eventually I get through, and head to the kitchen. The master-chef's missing, although I'm told he'll be back in five, so I wander into the cathedral. I don't normally do tourist-stuff. A grey-haired helper wobbles over, unsteadily.

"That's the white rabbit's door," he says, pointing across a grassy area to a wall with a small door in the middle. "Charles Dodgson wrote *Alice* here. Those were his rooms, and when pursued by a student he would dash back, slipping through there. The inspiration for the white rabbit's door."

"I'm late," I say.

The helper-guide is about to launch into a lecture. I quickly thank him and move deeper into the cathedral. There's a tomb in one corner, covered in stone ivy with peeping faces. Oxford is one of those places where history is deeply layered, no matter how ancient something appears, there's always something older buried inside. Overlooking the sarcophagus is an intricately carved wooden balcony, its steps worn away by thousands of worshippers. The sign states that this was the shrine of Saint Frideswide, built in 1289 to hold the relics of a Saxon lady who lived 700 years before the college was formed. I touch the carvings, and caress one of her many stone faces. Light enters through a stained glass, highlighting her smiling face in pale blue, dust motes swirling in the beams.

Ten minutes later I'm walking though the meadow, with a heavy bag of ice containing four live lobsters. It's hotter now, and the bag is dripping. I can feel the lobsters squirming. Strictly speaking, the creatures should be frozen for two hours to render them unconscious. Then we use a skewer to pierce the cross on their heads, conveniently placed to allow chefs to perform instant executions. That's current best practice for the humane preparation of shellfish. I don't have two hours. We'll need to handle this the old-fashioned way. The dean may be a stickler for ethics, but people don't get slowly numbed and terminated, we must face our exit, however and whenever it appears. If that's good enough for people, it should be fine for lobsters.

Our names are stacked under four spice jars with coloured lids, each matching the spot of colour we've dabbed on a lobster. One of them has a mis-shaped shell, and I daubed that one in blue, and set my name against it. Andy holds two and Steve has the yellow one lined up. They have ten feet to cover from table legs to the cooker, where the water is boiling furiously. Race for the pot.

"Are you ready?" I ask. Andy and Steve both assent, and one lobster clacks its claws on the floor.

"On your marks," I say.

If Blue wins, I tell myself, everything will be fine. My lump will be a minor issue that fades, a cyst maybe, something benign. I don't know why this thought occurs to me, but somehow, I completely believe it's true. My fate will be settled in the next sixty seconds. For some reason, I picture the elm tree filling the courtyard, sighing and shivering in the cooling air, stirring to take its part in the process.

"Go!" I shout.

Andy and Steve release their captives. There's no movement at first, as though the lobsters can't believe they're free. Yellow turns around, and Steve repositions him to face forward. Andy prods Green and Red takes the early lead, but Blue is in pursuit, and when Red pauses, Blue clambers on top of him, unsure whether to fight or mate. Green has started slowly but seems to be heading steadily for the pot in a determined fashion.

"Come on Blue" I say.

Andy and Steve encourage their chosen bets. Green keeps moving forward.

"Bluey. Come on Blue. You can do it."

It's crazy, I know. The fate of this armoured crustacean can't possibly have anything to do with my life, but now I've made the connection I can't break it.

"Bluey! Move it!" I start to swear. My voice rises in volume. Andy and Steve fall silent.

"Blue, Blue, Blue." I'm screaming, and I realise everyone has stopped, except Blue who is moving again. He cuts diagonally across the route, possibly to intercept Green. I yell at him. I see the dean's feet, shuffling forward. I glance at him, and his boiled-red face, then at the sheepish expressions of my assistants, but it's too late now. Bluey gets one claw across the finish line. I snatch him up and drop him in the pan. The dean yells, spitting fury. He moves towards the stove and I block his way. I don't really hear his words. I do hear the water bubbling, and as it sank, I was distinctly aware of the sacrificial hiss made by the blue lobster's shell. My attention is captured by the light that penetrates the window, filtering through the elm tree. The light is golden now, warm and encompassing. I smile at the dean as he rants and rages. Everything will be okay.

Katherine Wolfe

Night in the Library

On the library's second floor,
in an out-of-the-way-space,
there's a patchwork sofa,
green, orange squares
embroidered with leaves,
vines, trees against brown
suede-like fabric, a donation
by a well-meaning alum
unfamiliar with proper
library décor, a sofa
not liked by the librarians
but loved by the students.
Tonight a young man, navy
knit hat, silver thermos
in one hand, sits on the sofa,
back propped against its soft
pillows, his black laptop open,
keyboard resting on his thighs.
A young woman places her head
on his shoulder, stares at her metallic
blue iphone, her long purple nails
pecking the screen until she hears
a swoosh and her message is sent.
They do not look up as I, the librarian,
push my cart of oversized books,
Folio ND 200s, Latin American art,
toward the stacks.

Deborah H. Doolittle

In Winter's Library

These days don dust jackets,
rest sturdy patched-over tweed
elbows on each padded arm
of the dusky wingback chair.
Some books are bound to sleep
standing up. Dog-eared
and pressed cheek to cheek
with last spring's dog-faced
violets. Light, once pulled from
the spine, turns itself inside out,
remains pale on the glass
and cool to the touch.

No sleet of furry feet,
no flurry of riffed pages,
even the reader closes his eyes,
lets his place slip
into the realm where jungle cats
dream of palm fronds
and parakeets. In the tropics
only the leopard changes his spots.
Meanwhile, the tabby traverses
the floor on its personal carpet
of sunlight. The unheard words go
unobserved and yearning.

Pamela Zembiec

The Chair

…Life and death are one thread, the same line viewed from different sides." Lao Tzu

The room was lit by the bright sunlight coming in through the living room window. It was the window closest to the view of Chase Creek which fed into the Severn River. The living room was the best place in my entire house. I retained all the original hard wood floors and the center place of the room was an enormous red brick fireplace which kept the room nice and cozy on a chilly winter day. Anyone who ever walked in my front door would notice the fireplace even before they saw the beautiful views of the water through large bay windows. Its width expanded from the entrance of the house passing the master bedroom, bathroom then finally ending at the kitchen.

The room was different now than before our world was shattered. I had to replace it all. The furniture, the sunroom, the curtains, the paint on the walls and even the stair banister had all been transformed. I tried desperately to start anew in the house that was his. It was and would always be his house. He found it, fell in love with it and coaxed me into buying it. Our friends would call it "the million-dollar tree house." In the end, that's what it became as I couldn't bear to live in this place without him so I changed everything spending unnecessary money on fixations that I probably shouldn't have. Everything was gone with one exception…the chair.

The chair was a 1980's light purple felt lazy boy recliner. It was a pleasant purple, not one that looked like the character Barney, but a nice washed out light plum a bit darker then lavender. It had numerous buttons decorating the upholstered back with cushions so comfortable, the thought of sleep entered your mind as soon as you sat down. Your hand would automatically glide over to the right-side panel enabling you to grab its wood handle to recline and snooze away. I had witnessed this with him on several occasions and the picture of my husband sleeping in the chair became rooted in my memory forever.

The chair had traveled to many locations…Virginia Beach, Northern Virginia, California and its final resting place, Annapolis, Maryland. As I changed everything in his house, the thought of removing the chair never entered my mind. I once placed a chair cover over it, but the reach for the wooden handle wasn't automatic which took the wonder away. So, I left it. As is. It stayed in the living room strategically placed next to the right bay window overlooking the creek. I never sat in it. I only looked at it; remembering a time when life was happy. And then it happened.

The sun was shining through the living room window, it illuminated the chair in a way that made the fabric looked washed out or even faded by the constant exposure to bright sunlight. I didn't pay it any mind as I went about my day only glancing here and there through my house making sure the floor was swept and everything was nice and tidy. All had a place including Doug's chair. Our daughter, Fallyn never sat in the chair. She was just a toddler turning three in March. She was a climber by nature and according to our pediatrician was "freakishly strong". I never cared if she jumped on the coach or our beds, but she never attempted to jump on the chair.

I was cleaning up after lunch when I heard her giggling hysterically in the living room. It was just the two of us now in the house so I assumed the television was on and kept doing my chores. The giggling was followed by three-year-old words which I ignored until she said, "Hi daddy." I was startled by the sound of "Hi daddy." It couldn't be as her daddy was laid to rest over 2 years prior. Who could she possibly be talking to? My immediate thought was she saw someone outside who looked like her daddy, but I had to get to her quickly and see for myself. As I walked down the hall lined by the huge brick fireplace, the giggling intensified. She was so elated, I had only heard her chuckle like this when I tickled her and kissed her sweet face. My walk turned into a slow jog as I turned the corner and there she was on the chair. Her little body was straddled on the top of the recliner back as she looked into the air laughing and waving. Her legs pumped feverishly as she belly-laughed and moved her body back and forth while the chair rocked.

I screamed, "Fallyn, what are you doing?" as I ran over to the chair worried she would fall off the back. She instantly stopped moving, turned her head, looked directly at me and said, "I'm playing with *my daddy*." Could this be real? I always believed in the afterlife and was obsessed with mediums and ghost stories. I had also experienced things such as this, but only in my dreams and never actually saw Doug's spirit while completely awake. Fallyn's baby monitor had flashing orbs on its screen which started the night of her daddy's death. She played peek-a-boo with "someone" who no one else could see each night before falling fast asleep. This was how she ended up in my bed. The orbs were comforting, but terrifying at the same time. They flashed back and forth across the screen just like the ones in the show "Ghost Hunters." I refused to watch the screen any longer and still needed the comfort of knowing my daughter was safe, therefore she slept with me.

This was beginning to make sense. He couldn't play with her any longer while in her crib and now he had found another way. Doug always had a plan B. His spirit was determined in life and now in death.

"Fallyn!" I shouted. "Be careful! You could fall off the back!" With the hair on my arms standing at attention and goosebumps swelling all over my body, I quickly grabbed her off the chair while in midstride of her belly laughs. I turned her face towards mine, looked at her in the eyes and gently said, "Well, that's fine you're playing with your daddy, but now its naptime." I cradled her in my arms all with uneasy stomach, shaking hands and nervous energy. We walked into my bedroom which was now "our" bedroom and I steadily turned the comforter down to get us both comfortable. Fallyn turned her little body on its back and just stared at empty air. It wasn't the space high up in the air close to the ceiling where most would imagine seeing an angel or spirit, it was the area directly in front of her. Watching something I couldn't see.

For what seemed like forever, she glared with a huge smile as her eyelids began to grow increasingly heavy. I viewed with both envy and fear, wishing I could see what she was seeing. She then turned her little chubby cheeked face to me and said, "Mommy, daddies got to go back to his home now." I said, "Ok, tell daddy bye and tell him we both love him very much." As she turned her face back to the hollow space, she raised her right arm waving goodbye to air, but we both knew it wasn't just blank space it was the one person who meant everything to us in this world and now he was in another unknown place some believe to be heaven. She waved her little hand while softly saying, "Bye, bye daddy, bye daddy…" and as her words faded her eyes closed and she was fast asleep with eyelashes like his so long they touched the top of her rosy cheeks.

Deborah H. Doolittle

Running the Old Road

At last, where my past lies
behind me,
sloughed off
like an outdated skin
a snake sheds.

The shoulders are soft
and crumbling.
Weeds have inched
into the cracks. Wild flowers
dot the grassy margin.

When I look up, I see
clouds piled high on mountains
like laundry, heaps and heaps
of them, extending
to the horizon.

Just one of those endless,
thankless tasks I've performed.
I pass afield and a post
with a shank of barbed wire
coiling into a lariat.

I pass more fields,
a stand of tall pine trees,
hear the crows call out
as they drop from the branches
to the earth.

I see foot hills
in my future and a T intersection,
where the patient stop sign
waits for me to obey
its command to stand still.

Joan G. Gurfield

A Very Good War

New York, 1968

In the coffee shop on the corner near Lionel Blaustein's West Village office, Jeanne reviewed her notes. BARD — Blaustein, Arsenault, Ross, Donnell — had just won the prestigious Architecture Firm Award, and she was about to interview him for *The New York Times*. She'd read about his training, and the fact that he'd immigrated to the U.S., years ago. She'd ask who his greatest influences had been, how he'd met his partners. Standard stuff. In the course of the interview, some nugget would inevitably turn up that would focus the article and make it interesting.

He'd be available after six, his secretary had said, and the office would be quiet then, except for the secretary herself, and a couple of other architects who would be working late.

Jeanne strolled down the street past three teenagers in rainbow-colored tie-dye sitting on the steps of an old brownstone, smoking pot.

The firm's offices were in a charmingly restored building with black iron railings and ivy trailing from window boxes. Despite being almost a native New Yorker, she hadn't known that the streets in the area were zoned "commercial".

The reception area was all cherry-wood paneling, tall, columnar cacti, and, on the wall behind the desk, a large, red, yellow, and orange painting that could have been a Jackson Pollack if Pollack had been in a particularly good mood.

The secretary led her to Blaustein's office.

"Hello," she said, "Jeanne Travert, from the *Times*."

He glanced up from the papers on his desk, smiling. He was a handsome older man, maybe sixty-five or seventy, white hair brushed back from a high forehead, piercing gray-green eyes, not too many lines and wrinkles. His pale blue shirt was crisp and fresh-looking, even at the end of the workday. His desk was immaculate, except for one manila folder and three pens that looked like pricy Montblancs.

He stared up at her, and his face grew pale.

Marseilles, 1943

A tall, scruffy-looking young man dashed up the steps and into the American consulate. He was late for his appointment.

The line of people, even for those who had appointments scheduled, was long. "It takes an hour to go from here, where we're standing, to *there*," the anxious looking woman in front of him indicated three doors at the top of the stairs.

As he waited, he noticed an attractive blonde in a tight black skirt and high heels excusing herself several times, walking up the stairs to the right, bypassing the endless line of people. Good legs, he noted, automatically. Probably a secretary. She made it to the landing. As she opened the door to go in to one of the offices, she turned and smiled down at him.

He tried to contain his impatience as the line of people crept, ever so slowly, up the steps. If he didn't get out of Marseilles in the next week or two, he'd be screwed. Fewer and fewer boats were leaving. Visas were difficult or impossible to obtain.

When he finally made it into the correct office and presented his paperwork, the weary-looking man — the undersecretary — behind the desk asked for four additional copies of his visa application and two copies of his birth certificate.

"I don't have a birth certificate. I had to leave Germany in a hurry."

"I understand. It's not an uncommon problem," the undersecretary was firm but apologetic. "We'll need to know who your sponsors are in the United States. You have to have two of them, and we'll need six notarized copies of their Affidavits of Sponsorship and Support. Come back when you've gotten the correct papers. The earliest appointment I can give you is on the 29th at ten. When you arrive, just go directly to the other side of the building, so you won't have to wait quite as long."

The young man walked hurriedly down the street, away from the consulate, his dark hair flying wildly, his shoes scuffed from so much walking in the last few weeks. He knew that he looked a mess. He'd been a natty dresser, once upon a time, in Berlin.

He'd have to locate Kurt's forger again and spend money on more false papers. He'd been resisting doing that because his funds were running low, although Kurt had warned him he'd have to.

On the waterfront at the old port, people milled around, hoping for a breeze. It was lunchtime. Vendors sold bits of fried food to those who could afford it. Gulls and other seabirds squawked above the commotion, hungrily diving for any scraps that were dropped. He spotted the blonde from the consulate at the same moment she saw him. They smiled and moved towards each other.

"From the office," she said, laughing.

"Actually, from the stairs."

It was as though they knew each other. She took his arm, and they began to stroll companionably along the boardwalk, dodging in and out among the crowd.

"You're trying to leave Marseilles," she announced.

"As soon as possible."

"Just when we finally met," she joked, flirtatiously.

He figured, why not, and he kissed her. The surprise was that she kissed him back.

"I'm Dominique," she touched a hand to her chest. "Do you have a place to stay?"

It wasn't as odd or as forward a question as it seemed, since many of the people thronging the docks were trying desperately to emigrate, and hordes of others in Marseilles lived on the streets or in whatever temporary shelters they could find.

"I'll stay with you," he offered.

"Will we be lovers, or just good friends?"

"Lovers." He felt a responsiveness in himself, a quickening of interest. It felt good to feel something again.

"What's your name?"

"Lionel. What can I say? My parents liked it."

"It's not bad. Strong-sounding."

"I've always disliked it. But you can't get away from who you are." In America, he didn't want to be traced. Some obsessed Nazi might hunt him down because of the bombs he'd planted on railroad lines going to Germany. Unless the war ended. He planned to use the name "Pete" there. It was the most American sounding name he'd been able to come up with. All his paperwork read "Peter Johnson," which had a slightly ambiguous feel — it could also be Scandinavian or British or even German. The man at the consulate today hadn't questioned it.

"What do you do at the consulate?"

"I'm the undersecretary to the undersecretary," she joked. "The assistant to the American who does the visa interviews, deciding who will be permitted to go to the U.S. and who won't. My boss has an impossible job. Like playing God. So many people desperate to leave. So many terrible stories…."

"What did you do before the war?" he clasped her hand as they meandered along the waterfront towards her place.

"I'm married," she told him. "But it's nothing."

"It's not *nothing*," he couldn't hide his shock. "Where's your husband?"

"I don't know. He was in the army, but I haven't seen or heard from him in two years. He may have been captured or killed. Before he left, it wasn't good between us. We weren't in love, the way one should be. But of course, I hope nothing bad has happened to him."

He wished she wasn't married. Or that she hadn't told him.

They hung their laundry — the pitifully few garments that he had alongside her stock of frilly, silky, pink and white things — from a line suspended from her second floor apartment to a neighbor's, across the courtyard. She had an arrangement with the neighbor: every other day, one or the other of them would pull the line in on a system of wheels and pulleys. "We know each other's undershorts, she and I, but we're not friends," Dominique told him. "We blush a bit, when we encounter each other on the street."

After he paid the forger for the second round of papers, he was saving the rest of his small stash of money for when he got to the U.S. He didn't know what he'd need there, or when he'd be able to earn more. She understood. She wasn't as broke as he was. Her income paid for the apartment and living expenses, and after their first week together, she told him that she had a daughter, living with her parents in the country, and that she was supporting all of them. So they were broke together. They made a game of it.

She cooked the soup, pistou, a Provencal speciality, because the particular beans that you needed were in season. Although she complained that there wasn't enough sausage in it, the soup was delicious. Best of all, it lasted them for three days. When they could find fish, they made bouillabaisse. Or sometimes they just ate bread. They had both lost weight since the beginning of the war, but he swore that the thin lines and curves of her body were beautiful.

He confided in her, telling her most of what had happened to him since the outbreak of the war. After he'd escaped from Germany, he'd joined a Resistance group in France. He'd been one of their leading saboteurs, until the group had been betrayed. There were men hunting for him, so he'd fled to Marseilles. Although she knew his real name, they used "Pete Johnson" for him when they went out, just to be safe.

He had nothing to do while he counted down the days until his visa appointment, almost a month away, so during the week, when she was at work, he read or took long walks beside the Mediterranean. Some days, he went to the Jardin des Vestiges, near her apartment, and stared at the plants, fascinated by the symmetry of their structures. Green places soothed him, almost made him forget.

On her days off, they tried to pretend that they weren't in the midst of a war. They acted as if they were tourists, and visited the ancient basilicas, Notre Dame de la Garde, and the other sites. They wanted to go to the Chateau d'If, on a small island just off the coast, where Dumas had set his *The Count of Monte Christo*, but there were no boats leaving the city for pleasure trips. Anyone getting into a boat, even a tiny fishing boat, was suspect. They were stopped and had to declare their business. Papers were inspected, and people were routinely jailed for any slight infraction. They couldn't risk it.

They went to the Friday open-air market, where they ran into his friend Kurt, whose visa had finally come through. "See you in New York," Kurt told him. "I'll go every day to a Horn and Hardart's — a cafeteria — around 40th street — somewhere in the 40s — at seven in the morning. My cousin says the coffee is good and the food is cheap. You'll find me there, when you come."

Dominique was torn: she didn't want Lionel to go, but she knew he had to leave France before he was caught and taken away by the Milice — police who were cooperating with the Germans, rounding up Jews, rounding up anyone who was politically suspect.

She knew exactly what questions Lionel would be asked at the visa interview, and she prompted him about the answers he needed to write on the forms. They'd want to know if he had a police dossier, a prison record, any military records. He had to lie and say he wasn't Jewish. They were only accepting so many Jews, and the quota had been reached. He had to declare that his education had been completed, that he was prepared to work in the U.S., and that he wouldn't be a financial burden to anyone. He'd be required to take a physical examination at the consulate.

"If I'm denied an exit visa," he teased, "maybe I'll go live with your parents, in the country."

"You can't take such a chance," she grew grave. "The Krauts have their tentacles out, everywhere. Someone would betray you, maybe spitefully, maybe by accident. I won't let you risk it."

The discussion ended, as all their mild arguments did, in bed. Their weeks together were one long, laughing dream-time.

His appointment at the consulate was on a Tuesday. From her office, she watched for him at ten o'clock as the line of people snaked up towards the small interview room, and she managed to indicate him to her boss. She'd never asked a favor of the boss before.

After the undersecretary interviewed him and stamped a few papers, Lionel went into her small office.

"Yes, Mr. Johnson, we can definitely give you the visa," Dominique stamped one of the documents. She smiled up at him. "That's it. You can stop holding your breath, now."

"Will you come to New York with me?" he asked, suddenly serious, now that he knew he'd be able to leave. When she didn't respond immediately, he said, "Or come later, and meet me there?"

"I can't. My husband may return … my daughter is here in France, and my parents…. You'll be getting settled there, for a few months, and I'll be here, doing this… ," she gestured to her desk, piled high with visa applications. "But who knows what will happen? Perhaps, after the war?"

Once he got to New York, he never heard from Dominique. She had no address for him, because he had no address and he didn't know where his friend Kurt was staying, at first, just the vague location of a cafeteria. The post office in Marseilles, close to the place where he'd lived with her, returned the letters he sent her, marked "Unknown". The only other address he could think of for her was care of the consulate. When he wrote there, they said she'd left the job and moved, with no forwarding address. It wasn't unusual during the war: people were displaced or bombed out, with no way of reaching each other. He wondered if her husband had returned and if they'd reconciled.

In America, he felt as if he was finally able to breathe again. When the war ended, he decided to use his real name. He finished architectural school and then began to work, at first in a large firm, and then in a smaller one that he created with some friends. After a few rather lonely years, he found a wife. Margie was a Midwesterner. She didn't understand why he jumped whenever there was a loud crack as a truck backfired in the Manhatttan streets. She didn't understand why whenever he and Kurt saw each other, they drank too much and spent the evening toasting their old comrades. And Lionel didn't understand her fixation on shopping at Bergdorf's and Saks Fifth Avenue and her attachment to fashionable furs and pricey jewelry. After five years, they parted, not on the best of terms.

Afterwards, he had a couple of affairs. Nothing earth-shattering. He wanted what he'd had with Dominique: that easy-going, bantering kind of relationship, that even-tempered living together, but he didn't find it. Yet women had always found him attractive. And sometimes, he responded.

New York, 1968

In Blaustein's office, Jeanne asked, "Do you think your firm won the award on the basis of the well-known Ibica Museum, or on your entire body of work?"

He considered the question carefully before answering. "The awards committee seems to value a firm's body of work, at least that's what it's been like, the past few years. But you'd have to ask the committee members what went into their decision."

"Can you tell me a little about your life, aside from work? Do you have a family? Pets? A hobby?" So far, the interview was a dud. She needed to get something more out of him besides charming surface and blandness.

"Divorced, for many years. No children."

And then she said, "You're from Germany, originally. What made you come to the U.S.?"

"I'm from Berlin, which isn't exactly like the rest of Germany. I'm Jewish. I fled to France during the war, and then I came here, to New York."

She wanted to unlock whatever was behind his cool, imperturbable façade, "What happened to you during the war?"

"'How was your war?' as the Europeans say. I had — how should I put it — a very good war, at least, for a while, at the beginning. I don't mean that in any callous or insensitive way, just that I was one of the very few lucky ones. I was still in school when the war started. My parents had friends who helped us escape from Germany. My parents made a new life for themselves in England, but I stayed in France, working with the Resistance. And then, later, I was fortunate enough to get out of Europe in the nick of time. But there were so many I knew who didn't survive." His eyes teared up, and he looked away from her. "As if a war can ever be good. It's amazing, the human ability to compartmentalize: *me*, *me*, *me*, and *my* family, *my* relatives. Without thinking of the many, many others."

"I don't want to make you uncomfortable," she tried to probe delicately, "but is there anything particular you'd like to tell me about that time?"

He gazed at her for a long moment, and then shook his head,no. "You remind me so much of someone I used to know, a French woman."

"I'm French, by birth."

"Your English is perfect. Like a native speaker."

"My major was English. And journalism. And I've been here a long time. Who was the French woman you knew?"

"Her name was Dominique Gagne."

She flinched. "She's my mother."

He gasped, and his face turned white and then red. "She's the one who rescued me, who helped me leave France."

She stared at him, astonished. "That's… unbelievable!" Her mother had told her that she'd helped more than a thousand people leave France during the war, but he was the first one Jeanne had met.

"Is she alive, Dominique?"

"Yes."

"Is she well?"

"Very well. I was just over there to visit her two weeks ago."

"Where? Where does she live?"

"Lyon."

"Ah." He took a deep breath. "How old are you, if I may ask?"

"Twenty-eight."

"That would be about right. She had a little girl when I knew her. That must have been you. But how did you end up here, in the U.S.?"

"For a job." She didn't have to tell him about following Mark to New York or how their relationship had gone so disastrously wrong.

He nodded. "And what about your father?"

"He died many years ago. Henri Gagne. He was an engineer. My mother went back to using her maiden name after his death. She goes by Dominique Travert. And I took the name Travert, too." It was as if *she* was the one being interviewed. How was she going to shape all this into a piece?

"I was never able to locate her after the war."

"You tried?"

"I tried. Believe me, I tried."

"You knew her well?"

"I knew her…. She worked in the consulate in Marseilles."

"Yes, the visa section."

"She never mentioned me? Or a man, an American named Pete Johnson?"

"No. Not that I can recall."

"Is it possible….could you give me her phone number, her address?"

"Of course. I would write to her, first, though. It might be difficult for her to understand who you are, on the phone. Unless you want me to talk to her, first."

"No. I don't think so." His hand trembled on the desk. "Do you have a photo of her?"

"Nothing recent." Jeanne fished in her wallet for the photo of her mother. It was an old one, from when she was twenty or twenty-one.

"Yes." He looked at the photo. "Dominique," he pronounced the syllables slowly, savoring them. "Dom-in-ique."

She remembered, then, her mother saying, (oddly out of character, she'd thought at the time), when she'd told her she was thinking about moving to New York with Mark, "If you love him, *go*."

Bob Wickless

Road Building: An Elegy of Sorts

In memory of my father

You are with me today,
And we have walked out
Behind the house
To watch the highway crew
Building the new bridge.
Back on the yellow wall
In the kitchen you hand-built
The insurance calendar says
Summer 1958.
Now *it is* Summer 1958.
You are 61, I am not quite
A dozen eggs you say,
Fifty cents, a penny each
For the differences between.
Even so, you are filled
With the promise of these times,
The phrase
Some Chrysler ad executive coined
For Saturday night,
Lawrence Welk,
The forward look.

We walk along the hard-packed dirt
That will soon become
The road
To the crazy quilt
Of plywood and steel
That will soon become
The bridge.
You point out
How they use real cork
Between the joints,

How it is still the best choice
Even though it costs so much,
How, without it,
The finished bridge
Might buckle and split
As, over years, any surface tends
To expand and then contract.
You show me how
The bridge's heavy forms
Will soon peel off
After a 3 day continuous pour,
Revealing the final shape
Of the finished bridge.

Today it is Spring,
Always 1986,
4 months since
I followed you
Across that one place
For the last time.
Yet it is not
That single day, its odd moments
Placed outside of time,
But these small incidents,
One conversation
In a thousand, a million
Spoken over years,
To which I respond.
How they have taught me well
Your sure care with materials,
Your ability to teach
What any builder must know first—
What's constructed
Only to be later stripped away,
What expands, what contracts,
What, when it's revealed, remains
What we leave.

David Dixon

Dominion

She is small and wary at the new feeder
I brought home from the hardware store

and I use your mother's old field glasses
from 20 feet to study the outline

of her faint ruby crown,
the slight hint of an olive-green breast.

One eye, white-ringed, stares back.
She is an arrival of the new season,

and I linger in the notion
of a Distant Being so able to attract

and sustain
such tiny bundles of flight,

so influential of intention
in these many feathered comings

and goings, so benevolent
in the pretense of dominion

with the simple swipe
of a plastic card.

Yet even given my
grand provision of Spring,

I too have become
like this small and careful creature;

keeping one eye on the feeder,
and the other on everything

that might come
between me and wild sky.

Susan Williamson

The Mare Who Swam Backstroke

If pawing were an Olympic equestrian event, Footsie would have earned several gold medals. We didn't give her that nickname, she came with it. That should have been a sign. I remember seeing her shake an entire six horse trailer stopped in traffic on I-40. There was no question in my mind as to which horse was the culprit.

The first week we brought her home we learned she was a bit neurotic. When my husband led out her stable mate and prepared to work the other horse, Footsie began leaping, rearing, kicking and pawing to the point of possibly causing damage not only to herself and her stall, but the entire barn. In desperation he put the other horse away and worked her. All went well. The fact that her registered name was "Be Something" should have warned us that it was always about her.

She performed well in the show ring, but there was no letting her stand tied to the trailer while we showed another horse. Even with her lead in my hand, she was pawing, stomping and fussing. At one show my husband and I were planning to show in the same class. I was riding Footsie. As we warmed up, he would ride over to see how I was doing. Fine, until he came near on another horse. That was totally unacceptable. Footsie commenced bucking and shying and generally being unreasonable. Being concerned, he came closer.

I yelled, "Get away from me!" Exhibitors scattered and gave him sympathetic looks. I decided to scratch from the class and when my feet hit the ground Footsie flew backwards and almost into a moving truck, breaking her bridle in the process.

When we had both horses home and secure in their stalls, I went in to offer her a drink. She turned away as if to say she wasn't interested in anything I had to offer.

My husband laughed. "She's snubbing you."

One lovely fall day I decided to take my trail horse for a ride in the pasture adjacent to the barn. Footsie was turned out, happily grazing in the paddock behind the barn. When she saw me, she charged the gate at the bottom of the hill, intending to knock it out of her way. What she didn't know was that the gate posts were set in cement and not going anywhere. Beside the gate, a concrete stock tank provided water to three pastures. Boards spanned the top of the tank to separate the users.

Footsie hit the gate at a dead run. The gate did not move. But Footsie was flung up into the air and landed upside down in the stock tank, crashing through fence boards and causing a mighty splash. The horse I was riding was rather unnerved and my first job was to keep him under control and get him back to the barn so that I could see to the thrashing mare who had no doubt broken her neck or back.

"Whoa, Footsie, "I yelled," then "Easy, Rhythm, easy boy." Rhythm and I made it to the barn and I threw him in a stall yelling for my daughter to call my husband, our neighbor, anyone.

I ran to the mare. Her head was out of the water and broken fence boards spanned her belly. I knew that there was a drainpipe near the middle of the tank designed to take overflow after a rain. Was it sticking into her? I couldn't tell. The normally clear water was opaque from her thrashing. I pulled away the boards and tried to keep her calm. I ran back and forth from the mare to the phone on the wall in the barn looking for help. Finally she rolled herself around so that she was right side up. I ran back to the tank. She stood up. Scrapes covered her back and sides, but no apparent grievous wounds. With my encouragement, she politely climbed out of the tank and stood shivering in the October air. We grabbed towels and began to rub her down. I put a wool cooler on her and asked her to walk forward. She appeared miraculously sound. We rubbed and walked and I put in a call to the vet. We doctored her injuries—she had removed the hair from a large section of her back and side but was otherwise unhurt. The vet suggested a shot of antibiotic to ward off any potential infection. When she was almost dry and had stopped shivering we led her into her stall. My husband and a friend we had tracked down arrived about that time.

She was stiff for the next few days, but all of her scrapes healed quickly. The experience may have been a turning point in our relationship. She now regarded me as her co-keeper.

Many a nervous show horse has been comforted by a goat or even a rooster. Footsie had her own cat. It appeared in the barn one day, walking around the edges of her stall. When it sat on the feed trough, Footsie came up to sniff.

"Hiss, smack."

Footsie jumped back and slowly approached again. After a repeat performance the cat had her well trained. She would even allow the cat to jump down onto her back from the hayloft above.

We decided to breed her. We were watching "Free Willy" on the coldest night of the year when our son checked on her and informed us she was in labor. We had rigged heat lamps and bales of straw around the barn aisle to give her a large warm space. While most mares don't want anyone around during foaling, Footsie always insisted on our presence. She would get tired pushing and lie like a beached whale waiting for us to help.

She showed successfully in several divisions and became our daughter, Wynn's, 4-H horse. When our daughter showed her in hand she pawed and twisted and refused to stand still. Repeatedly, Wynn led the mare back into place, trying not to let the frustration show on her face. Winners were announced backwards from tenth place. When she hadn't earned a ribbon by fourth or fifth, we knew she was out. But then they called her number as the reserve champion, the judge saying, "This girl never stopped showing her horse."

One winter Footsie suffered a severe attack of colic. Horses can not vomit and intestinal distress caused by a blockage or twist is often deadly. Surgery can resolve the issue, but by the time you realize it is needed, it is often too late. For a day or two it was touch or go. She was happiest loose in the barn aisle so she could follow us around. She would stay close and lie down near us.

She recovered and went on to have several more foals. She worked as a lesson horse, cantering so slowly I could walk beside her as she introduced a rider to their first canter steps. She also took her riders to the center of the ring or somewhere else they didn't plan to go until they mastered her.

One might think she would be afraid of water. No. She loved it. Creek or mud puddle, she would stand pawing until all of the water was muddy and she was wet from head to hoof. I couldn't look at her without thinking about the stock tank.

She was twenty-seven when navicular disease left her so lame that the time had come to put her down. We all shed tears for the mare who had taught us so much.

Jaclyn Miller

Buffalo Hide

The kill was quick and we wanted to honor you
To use every part
On crostini, with honey and goat cheese,
Seared lightly
That heart, your heart,
Alive not long ago
That heart
Bleeding, beating, bleating
Now touching my lips -
I just couldn't coke it down
It tasted
Like life

I've met my own hunter
By name and shadow
His nails drag like daggers
Picking a thread from a loom
And in that tapestry of thoughts he plucks
The guilt and the anguish
Patterns of disappointment
Like bison on a rug
Under the feet of those who ruined them
The fake sun above the white herd
The sun shining bright amongst these thoughts
And a lace dress never worn

I picked lambskin for you
For you to lay upon in your crib
To sooth your mewl
And drumming heart
Soft fibers to lighten the shadows
That hunt us all to our extinction
-Only love to orbit you-
And I find myself now
In a circumvolution
Along with the moon and the hunter
And the skin
Empty of flesh

We should use every part
Like the earth does
Creating and recreating
Meat to grass to stomach
A thread casting a larger picture
Even the hide breaks down
Used as bedding and dolls
And bird's nests
Where young eggs are hatched
And sometimes broken
Sent back
To dissolve into the tree from which they grew

We put granite on top of you
To keep our imaginations at bay
To keep from visioning your
Skin and bones turning soft
From rising back up
From regenerating into lesser forms of you
Short bursts of blooms
Unequivocal to your
Short bloom
Blocking an idea – the thought
That the grass and wildflowers and roots
Might just drink you up

I was one Malbec bottle in
Caught up in melancholy
Remembering the way you smelled at birth
My mind stuck in that moment
The sudden smell of slaughter hit me
Smoke rising
In my cast iron, the remaining buffalo heart
Charred. Cauterized. A relic now.
It tasted bitter and sharp
Like death
And that, I could eat
Every bite

Stanley Moroncini

The Good Memory Book

In the evenings, he would hear their voices, coarse, full of regrets and memories that were stronger than his own. In the mornings, he could hear birds outside his hospital window, singing a song, mysterious to man. In the twinkling light of dusk the nurse would come in and change his bedding. She would check his vital signs, humming the same droll hum each time. She was Filipina, or so he thought, and her body was small and round, and her smile was warm but lacking character, as if she practiced it in a mirror until she got it right, a pre-packaged smile for the sad sack vets she cared for in the grey hospital that so many souls were chained too.

The nurse rarely spoke of anything beside the weather and the barely held together man that was her charge wondered if she were part of the doctors' experiment to revive what he used to be. What the brown leather-bound book sitting at the end of his bed like an attentive dog was supposed to help cure.

The nurse spoke of the coming chill of fall, the lessening of light and the tanning of the leaves. He remembered, or thought he did, the smell of fall. The air, thick with the scent of fireplaces, so crisp and cool he thought that as a child he could take a bite of it, and in that moment, savor the flavor of pumpkin and apple pies that added to the smell of the coming winter.

On the days he would sit across from the therapist he would notice how her eyes fought a losing battle with the side of his head, which still ached and throbbed, especially when the chill air the Filipina nurse spoke or found him as he wandered through the gardens of the veterans hospital, before an orderly or a nurse rushed out to grab him and take him back to his bed.

She was doing it again, the doctor who had given him the brown book, what she had described as "essential" to his therapy. He had caught her staring at the mound of purple contusions, mostly hairless, but patchy with thin, pathetic strands struggling to gain a foothold. The doctor looked away as he caught her and she readjusted herself on her seat and looked down at the yellow notepad resting in her lap. She cleared her throat and pushed the button atop her pen rapidly.

"What have you written?" She would say not looking up, her cheeks reddening.

"Written?" he would say.

The doctor, maybe as before, would point down to her patient's lap and would say, on the verge of sighing, "The book... your good memory book... did you write anything down? Has anything come back to you? About the time before?"

His eyes would glaze and his body was there but he was not. The plant in the corner of the room needed water and he wondered what type of color ink his pen was and the ceiling fan was too loud or did it need to be turned on and the doctor was a woman and what was she doing in the room?

"Henry?" the doctor would say.

Yes, his name was Henry and he was 23 and living in Seattle and he was a soldier who had been in a land where the sun was so hot and so brutal your skin would bubble and melt if you touched steel with an ungloved hand. A land where the children's eyes were filled with fear and hatred, a place where they fought an enemy that was never seen for reasons he couldn't remember, before the contusions had appeared on the side of his head.

A place where a man that he remembered as a friend and a brother who he loved, had disappeared in a flash and a bang. And then he was with a Filipina nurse who spoke of fall, or was it spring? And who the hell was this woman in the room with him and why were her eyes disapproving behind a set of black, thin-framed glasses?

"The good memory book," he said once to her. Or twice, or a thousand times.

"It's supposed to help you," someone had said. "You write down the good memories before the attack.... To help your memory."

At that he had picked up the book and turned it over. The leather was smooth and smelled of what he knew to be the interior of a car his father had once owned. A car he was not allowed to eat anything in. Henry remembered being frightened once, when he had spilled soda, or water, or coffee in the back seat. But his mother had come out to help him and shrugged her shoulders and said accidents happen. When they had cleaned up the mess she had hugged him and whispered in his ear, "No need to tell your father."

He felt her heartbeat and smelled her perfume. Her hair was soft as it always was, and in the moment her hair had caressed his face she had hugged him closer, tighter, and Henry knew he was loved.

There's something, he thought. A good memory.

He picked up a pen or a pencil and marveled at the browning leaves outside his window. As he opened the book with its volumes of blank lines he wondered what was for dinner and if the Filipina maid was coming to clean up his room and he thought of a man he had loved as a brother with a laugh that made all those around him, even the enemy they fought, be at ease.

"There's nothing to write," he told the doctor before, or after, or never.

She had stomped her foot at that, or thrown her pen, or nodded and looked down at her notes.

He opened the book once and saw a line scribbled in familiar writing, 'a single soul in two bodies.'

He wondered what that meant and someone in the hallway laughed at a joke he had missed the punch line to.

Outside the air was cold but he could feel the warmth of the heater in his room. Henry put pencil to paper and wrote about a staggered line of Humvees riding slowly out of an army base, of a turn in the road and a dead dog. How wiring stuck out of its butt and even the flies knew to stay away from it.

He stopped. Decided to change course.

Henry could have written of the sound, so loud it made his ears bleed. The concussion, how his teeth vibrated after the flash that blinded him. He could have written of the feeling of being picked up off the ground, how he felt suspended in the air as the steel around him buckled and groaned and the peculiar feeling of knowing he was going to make it came into focus as the steel world around him collapsed.

How his next thought coming in a thousandth of a second before the last was how Superman was a punk for getting beaten by a green rock, while he would survive this.

He could have written of the smoke and the fire, of the warmth of something oozing down his face and filling his mouth and how his left eye stopped functioning. How there were screams around him, and shooting and hands grabbing at him and the suffocating, lung burning powder from fire extinguishers.

But Henry did not write this, for somehow, he remembered, that this was a good memory book.

Henry wrote of the song they played in the vehicle at the time, the conversation he had with a man he loved who drove the truck, the sound of his voice as they turned the bend and a dog with wires came into view.

He wrote of Halloween as a child, of a Golden Retriever he named Sam, of summer nights as a teen, of a first kiss, awkward and thrilling in the same breath with a girl named Marie, he wrote of his mother, the softness of her hair, and his stern, emotionless, father who cried when his son told him he was going to war, and he wrote of the spring and the fall and the fireplace scented air, and the apple pie.

And finally, of a man who he loved who was braver and more noble then Henry could ever hope to be, who was gone.

The Filipina nurse came in and he put the book away and watched her set his meal down. She spoke of the weather again and when she met eyes with him, something she had never done for long, he put his hand on hers and asked,

"Who was I? Before the war?"

She took his hand in return and said, "you were Henry."

Jaclyn Miller

Oysters

I feel trapped by beige. Walls of grey and old wallpaper.
Florescent lighting. Sometimes I need the swelling beach.

Or the green found on a magnolia leaf or moss twined up a
Live oak branch. Put it in a picture frame, right next to yours

Wrapped in golden, a delicate skin, a husk hiding flower.
Amplify and ignite. Fireworks the day before the

Fourth. Sudden and unexpected and just as brilliant.
All shades of dinnerplate dahlia. Graceland and American Dawn.

Spartacus Orange. Bloom for us – our eyes only.
Fixed and saline still. Waves and waves and waves

Of color and pain and pleasure. Swaddled sweetly
In earthy soil. That scent of truffle and wildflowers

Of smoked lamb burning into our nostrils. That
Lukewarm flesh and lively blood on a white platter.

An offering, when there is nothing to offer. Only quiet
Words and florescent lights that bumble in hallways

And your hand on my forehead. Eyes like the
Ozark sky at midnight. Hills surrounded by shadows.

Expansive and laced with lights. An undulation.
A surge of neon and black. Of inferno and hailstone.

Orbit and flux. Changed and unchanged in one brackish
Mouthful. A colossal expression. To bray and to buck on the

Barren fields under our feet and still manage to grow

Something at all. To strangle the sand and influence the

Tide to bring us pearls amongst our shipwrecks.
And we both pray for soft landings and lambs

In meadows. Changed and unchanged. Hardened
And softened, somehow. And still in love with

The vibrant colors of life. As the white oak turns
Her leaves into wings. As the dogwood sheds its

Buds into the wind. Snowstorm in spring.
And our plastic flowers, as tender as the real thing.

Maybe even more so, though they look calloused.
Such little oysters we are. Briny and stoned

And full of muscle and flavor and grit.

L. G. Pethe

War Zone

It could have been any of a thousand young voices…

Couple of my buddies gettin' killed. They saying that's more or less a war zone, that's where everything happen, right there. Don't too much happen back here. It happen back here, but it don't happen as frequent as down there by the field. People get beat up a lot down here, but people get shot and killed there, get dead and put on ice down there.

1:00 a.m. Two blocks over, a police car whines down Chicago Avenue. Slate-grey buildings huddle against the night. A streetlight casts a pool of light on the sidewalk. A boom box perches atop a parked car. The music hammers an endless beat, holding city night sounds at bay. *Thump thumpa thump-thump.*

Five young black men face off. Three of them are yelling at the other two. The words flail. Eyes scream. The center man in the trio convulses with each insult he fires. A gun trembles in his hand. The two soon-to-be victims, arms at their sides, inch back against the chain link fence.

Thump thumpa thump-thump.

A car pulls over to the curb. A window rolls down. The driver shouts a name. One of the lesser in the trio turns his head, squinting at the car. A door opens. A middle-aged, white man emerges from the vehicle. The ankle-length, blue robe he wears whispers along the sidewalk. The two youths on the fence look at the man, eyes questioning.

The man strides to the group, positioning himself between the trio and the duo. The gunman quiets. The man, talking gently, extends his hand, lying it atop the hand that holds the gun. The trio members look at one another, unsmiling. The gunman relaxes his arm, letting the weapon drop to his side. Then he jams it into his jacket pocket.

Thump thumpa thump-thump.

Brother Bill Tomes breathes deeply. The gunman cracks a slight smile. He gestures and the victims flee. This night, the body count will be lessened by two.

In the words of a young friend of Brother Bill…

When I first met him, I thought he was the law. It took me probably about three months to know him and everything. When I see him standing out there and letting 'em get shot out, when they was shooting and he was still out there, I knew he wasn't no police. So I said, like okay, he must be doing some good in the neighborhood.

Brother Bill Tomes works the streets. He spends much of the night driving between Chicago's housing projects. Cabrini Green Homes. Henry Horner Homes. Robert Taylor Homes. Rockwell Gardens. The names are signposts for Chicago street violence, gang warfare and a host of urban social ills.

"Well, we're primarily concerned about the violence in the neighborhoods," says Tomes. "We go out there if there is shooting. We stand directly between them. I've been shot at twenty-eight times." With heavy glasses, grey hair edging his receding temples, he looks more like a Catholic grade schoolteacher than a gang mediator, a dodger of lead. "Even guys who are involved in the shooting or are going to get involved on a particular night—they'll say, 'well, at eight o'clock, we're going to be doing this.' They wouldn't say that unless they halfheartedly wanted you to be there," Tomes concludes.

He works for the Brothers and Sisters of Love, a mission out of Evanston, Illinois, where Tomes grew up. It seems a strange contrast. This squeaky-clean, middle-class community being home base for Tomes' nightly sorties into nearby Chicago's war zones.

"I asked a priest one time why God didn't choose a holier and wiser and older man than myself for this work. The priest said, well, the people would look at such a man and say what a fine person he is—but we're not like him. Whereas gang members look at you and say, well, he's just the same as we are—and he's trying. And that might help them to try a little as well."

A night voice confirms that…

Everybody over there loves Bill, everybody. That's why every time you see him pull up you see everybody come running to the car. I love Bill a lot. You know he cares for everybody over there.

Ninety-three of Tomes' friends in the projects have been killed. Their ages ranged from five to 25. Tomes tells of how one day at Cabrini Green Homes, two 10-year-olds approached him and asked if he was coming to their funerals. "So children in violent areas think about death as a daily reality," Tomes says.

A gang of psychologists at nearby Erikson Institute for Advanced Study in Child Development spends much of its time observing the effects of that reality on youngsters. In the projects, virtually all children have had firsthand encounters with shootings by age five. Twenty-five percent of all 15-year-olds have witnessed a homicide.

"They want to get out of the projects, want to get away from the environment," Tomes adds. He helps youngsters do that, if only for a day. "We go down Michigan Avenue, go to a park, go to the Great America theme park, or, on occasion, go over to Notre Dame on the South Shore commuter train." He believes the excursions give young people hope. It is a chance to see something different, a chance to expand their worlds. "They see that people aren't running around with guns, they're not shooting and things like that," says Tomes. "When they go back home, they think maybe they shouldn't be doing that either."

Post-Traumatic Stress Disorder is what the psychologists call it. It sets in after a child witnesses a traumatic event, such as a beating or a shooting. If a child has only one such experience, he or she usually gets over it. But it's different for kids growing up in the projects. They witness violence again and again. Over the long term, they look for ways to make sense of the world so that the acts of violence make sense. So they look for ways to become powerful, strong. They become prime recruiting material for gangs, which offer that strength.

As one recruit put it…

My friends, we just listen in and they be talking about going shooting and all that. So when I got a little older, we got our own gang, there was about six of us. We was running around and there wasn't no pressure on me. I did it 'cause I thought this was all that was up in the project. So finally, they said, okay, we're going to make you our baby Disciples. So that's how I got into the gang of Disciples.

For most children of the projects, the future is diminished. They don't say, "when I grow up." They say, "if I grow up." According to Tomes, their views of the world become shortened and focused on becoming powerful, on surviving the threats. The psychologists report that such children lose their sense of fear, resorting to dangerous acts and risk taking—like jumping in front of trains—as well as partaking in drugs and alcohol. This behavior gives them some respite from the fears that loiter in the backs of their minds.

Brother Bill's approach plays on that mindset. "Gang members get bored in the projects, so they decide to do a little shooting. If we stand between the gang members, they feel like somebody loves them enough to die for them—and that is emotionally satisfying for them. They think it's another kind of game, which can be as exciting as killing somebody," he notes.

Another voice in the night puts things into perspective…

A lot of us take for granted what we have. We really don't appreciate it 'till it's gone, when it's too late. Losing my first brother—that really showed me how much we take what's around us for granted. That's given me a lot of strength 'cause I'm in touch with reality and I know that from one minute to another, what you have can be taken away from you.

1:30 a.m. the young men slap hands with Brother Bill. He climbs into the car, says goodbye through the open window, pulls slowly away from the curb. In the rear-view mirror, he watches, listens as the *thump thumpa thump-thump* fades into the chorus of night sounds.

Mark Caskie

Aunt Eva and Aunt Annie, 1915

With sixteen stippled trout strong
across a plank you had outdone
all the men. It had made little difference
to your father since he had wanted
boys. Still, there were the young men,
and so before you allowed them
to take a photograph of your
catch, you changed into long white
dresses, with loose-fitting blouses
and bows at the neckline.
In the picture, you have drawn
your arms quietly behind you.
Aunt Eva, you didn't even look
at the camera, as if embarrassed
by your beauty, or
believing gentleman caller would
tease you over this photograph.
Aunt Annie, you look directly out,
satiric, as if you could chock
any evening full of laughs.
What response did you make
to the jokes of men,
over the prodigious bit of luck
that could bring such a catch?

If only they had seen you casting
your lines along the sunken logs,
or the way you baited your hooks without
flinching, the way you washed the blood
off your hands before returning.

Trish Sheppard

Topping

A sea of spikes
white and purple
crown tobacco plants

I inch down rows
peer across the field
blossoms, everywhere blossoms

one plant at a time
morning till evening

Close to the last leaf
I bend blooms in half
Snap
flowers tumble
lower leaves left to grow

On to the next and next and next
fingers—black with sap
twist, snap
plant after plant
row after row
until the last row
last plant

Dew covers my overalls
ocean boat blue denim
red patches on the knees
Fingers cramp
I look for row's end

I tie cloth pouches
over chosen spikes
seeds trapped
in cloth purses
ready for next year's crop

I turn and face
the farmhouse door
Hope for cornbread
and buttermilk
speeds my steps

I reach the front stoop
shake the dirt from my shoes
wipe my handkerchief across my face

The door opens
Ma smiles
"Wash up
Dinners waiting"

I use borax
on my hands
the sap clings
around my nails
and knuckles

I crumble my cornbread
into the buttermilk
eat a bite or two

My head drops
I start and jerk awake
My chair scrapes

as I push back

I weave down the hall
crawl into bed
close my eyes

Visions of plants loom——
one more purple spike
Snap
blossom after blossom
scattered on the ground
until sleep brings row's end

Landis Wade

Tried and Convicted

One of my handlers told a detective that I had some bad shit go down in my personal life and that's why I hate the court system, but that's the trouble with what's true and what's not. People believe what they want to believe. They can't get their heads around how a 96-year-old woman from deep in Appalachia with but ten years of schooling could be a fixer for 54 years and make a gazillion bucks doing it. I'm not crazy and that's a fact. Clever is totally and absolutely different than crazy.

Once upon a time, when I was young and pretty, I knew this handsome boy. He wasn't white like me, but I didn't care. He was kind, unlike daddy, who, in his small-town Baptist way, said I was a whore for getting pregnant at 14 and would go to hell. You were supposed to have sex for one purpose and one purpose only, except not before marriage, and definitely not with a colored. Two days after the baby was born, the boy I loved became what the law called a missing person. Daddy said he skipped out on me and was right happy about it. That smirk of his got me mad at men for the rest of my life and made me who I am.

Two years ago, I decided of my own accord to move into a cell-like room with faded lime green walls. The place smelled like feces and urine, masked only slightly by rubbing alcohol, but according to the doctors and judges, my stay was going to be short-lived, for monitoring and treatment, or death, whichever came first. The children – not the baby – were the ones who put me there, or so they thought. They told the court my mind wasn't right. The fact is, they didn't understand why, at age 42, after Sam died, I wanted to make my own way – without a man for once – and why I left this backwoods town for 52 years, only to return two years ago. "Mother," they whined, "why do you move so often?" I laughed at their stupidity. They had no idea what I did for a living and didn't know that a fixer has to live in the same place for a few years to get on the jury list and a few years more to get summoned for duty and that it's important to become embedded in the community, because they don't call the jury a panel of one's peers for nothing. All of which is to say that every time I moved to a new city, I assumed a new identity and I rarely called the kids, something they didn't like, so they called me on my 94th birthday. "Come home, mother," they said, "we'll have a party for you." Some damn party. More like an ambush.

We met every Thursday afternoon, the twelve of us, on the West facing wing, led by one of the handlers, an eager young She-Doc. Group was the same disjointed shitshow as the jury, because doctors are more like judges than they care to admit, telling people when and where to sit, how to think and what to do. The only difference between doctors and judges is the color of their robes. I saw the sessions for what they were – total bullshit – which is why I was so good at my job. I used those sessions to practice what I do best, forcing eleven other people to decide things the way I wanted them to be decided.

I remember this one session when Mrs. Russell Stanton Hamilton, IV explained another one of her many problems to the group. With her squeaky voice and tear stained cheeks, she told how her late husband had gambled their fortune away and kicked the bucket without paying his life insurance premiums. I tried to ignore her, but you can't ignore fingernails on a blackboard, so I had to speak up. I reminded her that Russell IV was dead as road-kill and never was any good to her to begin with and she should – no, she could – be her own person, solve her problems and even get laid, again, if that's what she wanted. I didn't tell her to change her given name, even though that would have helped my mood tremendously. I hated the name Beatrice with a passion, like the woman was a rodent in a children's book. To set her straight, I offered her some "be your own person" BS and asked her some Socratic-like questions – a trick law professors pull with their students when the professors don't know the answers to their own damn questions – because the key, whether in group therapy or the jury room, is making people think they are deciding for themselves. When the She-Doc asked Beatrice to make a decision –judges call that the verdict – the rodent came up with the well-formed answer I had planted in her head, and as I expected, the remaining heads in the circle nodded their approval. Case closed.

I don't like to brag, but I have to say that I've fixed some pretty high-profile jury cases. O.J. doesn't have a pot to piss in now, but back then, he had some serious cash hidden away and he used it to engage me for his not guilty verdict. I played the part of an old white racist, easy to do given the town that raised me and I became the reverse barometer for the truth. By the time I made my argument to the other jurors that the bloody glove definitely fit, the entire jury hoped I was wrong. I slipped a note to Johnnie Cochrane that said: "If it does not fit, we will acquit" and the rest is history. I cried like a girl when the others pressured me to vote for O.J., a performance worthy of an Academy Award. But, hey. I got something better, a shitload of money.

My favorite trial was the one where the government charged Lorena Bobbitt with cutting off husband John's penis. As was typical of 99 percent of the male population, the males on the jury wanted to blame the female and it really pissed me off. All the women thought Lorena perfectly sane for whacking off John's dick for raping her over and over, not temporarily insane, which is what we needed to decide to spring her. The hens cackled and the roosters flinched when Lorena told how she drove off that night with John's dong clutched tight in her hand only to toss it into a field. We laughed even harder about the case of the missing penis and what the 911 operator must have broadcast to cause a bunch of heterosexual men in uniform to spend their evening chasing dick. The story had the rapist in stitches, too, because after the cops found his little buddy, the docs rubbed it with antiseptic and sewed it back on in a nine hour operation. They did such a good job that ole John bounced back as a porn star in the movie titled: "John Wayne Bobbitt: Uncut." I kid you not.

Sequestered as we were in a two-star hotel, I hired a local hooker to pleasure four of the five misogynists and she got the fun on tape. The fifth wheel – the self-righteous preacher –balked at my generous offer, but only because he was a closet homosexual, a fact which came in handy when I threatened to expose him to his congregation at the Piney Grove Baptist church, where dancing was still a sin. In the end, we women voted to find Lorena Bobbitt not guilty by reason of an irresistible impulse, a legal term that means she could not control her actions even though she knew them to be wrong. And all the men on the jury who'd lost control the night before, plus the preacher, said "Amen," or was it, "Oh, God." Either way, the jury was satisfied.

Sex cases showed up in our group, too. The most memorable one was called "the case of the sexual inquiry," where Terrance Heart, a piston-pumping sex machine at age 91, started off by proudly reporting that he'd had sex with all the women in our circle except me, which was true by the way, because I'd sworn off sex after my fourth husband. The women in the group affectionately referred to Terrance as "Hardiplank" after that fiber-cement siding they use in construction that comes in long, horizontal strips and is almost indestructible. Hardiplank hoped the women would share how they felt when he was laying it to them, as he liked to say, and what kind of things they'd like done to them the next time around. Hardiplank had a tiny black book cupped in his left hand, a pen in his right hand and half-spectacles perched on his nose ready to record the answers, and I swear, the son-of-a-bitch had a boner. When She-Doc noticed, her mouth fell open, which was not the best visual for Hardiplank, but before he could perk up any more, Beatrice, having found her confidence, grinned from ear to ear. "Well," she said, "I'd like to say that when you touched me here…" She pointed to each breast with each forefinger. "On your nipples, you mean?" Hardiplank used a clinical tone as he made notes in his book, like he was her gynecologist or something. "Yes," she said, "that was very nice, but I think it was best when you used your fingers to…"

"Whoa, honeybun" I said, "let's save that for your exit interview." I still couldn't shake the memory of walking in on their finger-licking fun and didn't need a refresher. What I needed was a diversion, but She-Doc was no help. With her mouth still open, she could have caught a week's supply of flying protein, so I stepped in and called the question.

"Much as I'd like to know how much wood our good friend Hardiplank gave each of the women in our circle, I'd suggest we vote on it." I knew what they were thinking. Vote on what? It's called misdirection. Fixers do it all the time.

"All in favor of finding Hardiplank guilty of having the biggest swinging dick on the ward, raise your hand." The hands of eight women and two men shot up, along with my hand, which meant we had one hold-out, which is typical in the jury room, too. Wilson Peterman had his large hands in his lap with a frown on his face. "Mine's bigger." His tone was matter-of-fact, not angry. Come to think of it, I'd heard about Wilson Peterman's dick and the reports were quite lengthy, so I had to use my guile, because it takes twelve votes to seal the deal. I thought fast about the trial I'd had where the court appointed a third-party expert to make a recommendation to the jury. "I have an idea," I said. "I propose that Beatrice take matters into her own hands, report back on which size matters most and that her recommendation be final." Beatrice, Hardiplank, Peterman and eight other heads smiled and nodded and the case was closed.

I never told the group why I hated the court system and I won't say much about it now, but I will say this. When my third ex-husband took me to court, I got my ass handed to me. I had to start over, with no alimony, no house, no car and no source of income. My ex's fishing buddy was the judge and he ruled that the pre-nup – a wedding day surprise thrust at me by my rich bitch of a mother-in-law and the reason I got fucked twice that day – "is a valid and binding contract." He said it like he was scolding a child, so the next thing I did was run for judge against the bastard and I won, because nobody knows who to elect as judge, anyway, so it might as well have been me. Not long after taking the gavel, my patience ran thin and I got into hot water with the Judicial Standards Commission, because it became pretty clear to the entire state bar that I hated lawyers. The Commission griped about some petty ethical shit like cussing out lawyers in the courtroom, being late and drunk for work and having sex with two young bailiffs at the same time on the chief judge's desk. The chief judge – a high-browed lawyer – loved to brag about her imported desk and for that reason alone, I was fine with the outcome. Plus, being a judge was a good education. It trained me to manipulate trials. I quit before they could fire me, swiped left on Tinder, found Sam and married for the fourth-and-thank-God-final-time.

The kids salivated over Sam's $850,000 IRA and the two-bedroom, the spoils of his life's work. They felt it should come to them. He was their father, after all, and they never liked the fact that a 40-year-old thrice-divorced woman married their 75-year-old father and stuck her nose into their Norman Rockwell lives by having sex with their daddy in mommy's bed. They thought I was after his money, but little did they know that I was after his honey. Sam-the-man seduced me with some good ole-fashioned, bed-thumping, headboard-rocking sex and with that performance, I said "yes, I do." Sam was an addict. He really liked sex. Probably too much. It killed him six months into the marriage. Heart went out, with a bang I might add. And despite my grief, the children blamed me, as if it was my fault he liked sex more than his kids. No. Come to think of it. What they really didn't like was Sam's will. He cut them out and left everything to me.

The competency hearing the kids engineered 54 years later was their effort to gain control over Sam's assets and put me away, with the hope that I would die, soon. That morning, I went to the courthouse early and met with the clerk. I complimented her dress and let it slip that I had always wanted to serve on a really important jury case. "Do you think we will ever see such a case here?" I knew the answer when I asked the question. My handlers had reported that the case had been filed under seal a few weeks earlier and the clerk of court had just received the court's order to publish the allegations to the world that afternoon. The clerk smiled and patted me on the shoulder. "You never know." Hell, I knew. I knew it would take two years for the lawyers to posture and get the case ready for trial and knew that she would remember me. I thanked her and took the elevator to the third floor where I surprised everyone in the courtroom by agreeing to a two-year incompetency commitment.

The truth is, after traveling the country for over half a century, I came home to live with the mentally aggrieved as part of a well-crafted plan. The defendant in the case, a liberal named Robert Baxendale, had had enough of his only daughter who'd taken up with Jimbo Hadley, a local white politician who loved to talk about God and country and who spent his days hating on foreigners, gays, blacks and others he thought had similar genetic defects. Jimbo preached that Medicaid and Welfare were socialism, it was time to stop crying about Jim Crow spilt milk, and all programs for the poor should be eliminated, even though he was all for bailing out the banks, giving tax breaks to white private schools and propping up medical insurance for those who could afford it. Emma Mae Hadley, the one and only heir to the Baxendale fortune, was Jimbo's ever-loving wife, a two-faced bitch who didn't start visiting the person she called her "Commie-loving daddy" until after he won the state lottery. That suck-up maneuver pissed Baxendale off more than her marrying Jimbo and with every right by law he had coming to him, he cut Emma Mae out of his will and gave his 100 million dollar estate – which came to him through Powerball winnings and good investment advice – to the local zoo.

The lawyers for Emma Mae called Baxendale crazy, but who could blame him with such a spoiled bitch of a kid. If I'd had a daughter who'd sucked up to a prick like Hadley, I might of hired Lorena Bobbitt to cut the problem in half. And speaking of male genitalia, I was drawn to this case by the fact that the case caption – Hadley versus Baxendale – has important significance to anyone who ever attended law school. The same case caption appeared in the most famous case in English contract law. It involved the creation of a rule of law in a case where one party delivered a defective crankshaft to another party that they had planned to use to grind grain. But that's not the part law students find compelling. In the early 1970s, a first time actor assumed the porn name Hadley V. Baxendale – he probably did it to pay back his law school loans – and used his own crankshaft to drill Marilyn Chambers in the movie that launched the adult film industry, "Behind the Green Door." Again, true story. I couldn't make this up if I tried.

Emma Mae hired a brood of tall-building lawyers from the state capital to represent her and paid the local newspaper a wad of cash to print stories that her late daddy was Looney Tunes for giving all his money to otters and bears, but shit, it wasn't her money. If ole Baxendale wanted to give it to the animals, more power to him. I'm sure it's written somewhere in the Constitution that you have the right to put your life savings in a trash compactor if it makes you happy, no matter what your kids or their lawyers have to say about it. That's why when I was released from the hospital, I did the unusual. I cut a deal with Emma Mae to fix the case for her.

This was the biggest case I'd been a part of since I was a teenager. The courtroom was filled with townies and tourists and the press hovered like flies on stink. Thirty minutes before the evening recess, the lawyers had agreed on all but one juror. That's when the clerk caught my eye, winked and called my name. It was showtime.

Emma Mae's lawyers asked me questions first but knowing I was on their payroll, they accepted me as juror number twelve a few minutes into the conversation. The suits who represented the Baxendale estate became suspicious. Now it was their turn.

"Ms.…uh…Justice?"

"Please call me by my full name."

"Ms.…uh…Liberty-Anne Justice?"

"Yes, sir." My smile was a mirror image of the judge's frown.

The suit regained his composure. "Do you believe you can be fair and impartial about the sanity of a man who bequeathed his entire 100 million dollar estate to the local zoo?"

"I do."

"The other side says Mr. Baxendale should have given all his money to his daughter, not to the zoo. What do you think?"

I wanted to say that the bitch didn't deserve a dime but the judge might have thrown me off the case. "I think we need to consider all the facts before deciding someone is crazy."

"Ms. Justice, one last question." I sat up straight.

"How do you feel about the allegation that Mr. Baxendale was crazy for what he did?"

My entire plan boiled down to this moment. It's why I committed myself to the state hospital. I had wanted to know everything there was to know about living under the control of white-coated wardens, to feel and understand first-hand what it was like to be treated as if you were crazy, so that I could talk about it with conviction.

"Sir, I…"

For effect, I grabbed a tissue from my purse. When my eyes began to water, I spun my lie, the one I'd practiced, as truthfully as I could.

"Sir, I had a close friend – she was like a sister to me – who was wrongfully committed to a mental institution when she was only 16 years old." I told about the awful living conditions, "from the sour, antiseptic smells to the so-called doctors who pumped her body full of mind-numbing drugs." I told about how her black boyfriend, the father of her baby, had been lynched, how the police did nothing about it and how the lawyer prosecutor, with the help of the chief of police, convicted my friend of killing the lynching bastard. "They claimed she was crazy for shooting her daddy." I explained how the court stole my friend's baby and her inheritance, ruling she wasn't fit to be a mother and couldn't keep her daddy's money cause she'd knocked him off and was out of her mind. I made one thing clear, that she was "no more crazy than me."

I paused and wiped tears away from my eyes and off my cheeks. I'd practiced this, too, but I have to admit, the act left me an emotional wreck. When I was able to stop crying, I pressed my dress down in front of me and finished. "Sir, I'm an old woman who has been through a lot, but I promise you that I will follow the court's instructions and take seriously the question of whether a person should be judged crazy for doing what they believe is the right thing to do."

The rest of the trial was pretty straightforward. I did what I do best and turned the jury. But not in the direction Emma Mae expected. Having banked the ten million dollars for Emma Mae's side of the case, I cut a deal with Baxendale's team for another twenty million. With that deal done, I went to work and convinced everyone on the jury of the economic value and civic pride for our town of having "the best damn zoo in the U…S…of…A."

After the trial was over, I thought about moving to another state, but I'd gotten used to life on the ward and believe it or not, I missed the likes of Beatrice, Hardiplank and Peterman, and since I was 96 years old and had done most of the damage I could do to the court system, I voluntarily checked myself back into the hospital.

Two weeks later, I was on my laptop moving money around among my offshore accounts when a detective from the local police department showed up. We exchanged pleasantries while he glanced at the autographed photos of O.J. and Lorena on my wall.

"May I ask you a few questions about the Baxendale trial?" The detective tried to appear nonchalant, like I wasn't his target, but I knew I was, because Emma Mae and my handlers were pissed at my betrayal. But hell. I was 96-years-old and he was no Columbo. Plus, if the truth did come out, I would be known as the oldest criminal genius of all time, so I said yes and invited him to sit on my twin bed while I took a seat in my rocker.

"Do you know why someone would say you were on the jury in the Baxendale case?"

I smiled to myself when I realized the disguise had worked. That was one point in my favor. "I don't have the slightest idea."

"We got an anonymous tip saying you bribed the jury."

I laughed as I looked around the room. "With what? Pictures of celebrities."

Before he could ask another question, one of the He-Docs walked into the room. "Time for your medication." The prick said it with a smile, but it was not the kind you returned. It was one of those starched smiles, like he was on the same drugs he forced me to take.

The detective looked to the He-Doc and then to me. "Do you mind if I ask your doctor about your diagnosis?"

"Fine with me," I said. I picked up my yarn and needles and pretended to knit. I hate to fucking knit, but it's something old people are supposed to do, so with my hands occupied and my head tilted toward the window, I rocked, knitted and listened, because I am a much better listener than knitter.

My handlers had promised they would expose me if I ever betrayed a client and the He-Doc got right to it. He launched into a diarrhea-like spiel that included words like "delusional" and "court system" and "jury tampering" and "therapy" and "boyfriend" and "pregnancy" and "lynching" and "murder." The detective eyed me with what looked like sympathy while the He-Doc talked.

"She has no living relatives. Her only visitors are a young pastor and his wife from the local Baptist church who she thinks are her step-children." The He-Doc said it like it was the solution to an Agatha Christie mystery. Obviously, the kids were Baptists, like their grandfather and everyone knows that dipshit step-kids of the Baptist variety don't count as relatives. But He-Doc was one of the handlers who never believed in my work, so it wasn't hard for him to lie.

I heard the detective ask a question about my court system obsession and the He-Doc leaned over and began to whisper, poorly. I heard every false word. He left out the truth and blathered on with some made-up story about me having lost the only two people I ever loved in my life, one by hanging and one by court-ordered adoption to a family in Detroit. The He-Doc said I didn't trust judges and lawyers and hated cops, which is true, but not for those fairy-tale reasons, and he said I had been a ward of the state for 80 years. Hell, this He-doc couldn't even count – it had only been two years – but the detective was buying his lies, so I ignored them both, and continued rocking.

When I feel sad, I close my eyes and rock. Rocking soothes me, makes me content, not that screwing the court system for the last 54 years hasn't given me immense joy, it's just that I like the back and forth motion. It reminds me of when my mother rocked me at night as a little girl, and of the few days in the hospital when I rocked my little girl, when there might have been a happily ever after. I try to remember what followed but it's hard. My handlers call it blocking, but I don't think that's it. I think I have a broken past that never healed. It's why I became a fixer.

"Did you understand what the doctor said?"

I stopped rocking, leaned back and looked the detective in the eyes. I understood perfectly what the He-Doc said and true to my plan, I had nothing to fear now and nothing more to say, because my secret life as a jury fixer was safe. For a moment, neither the detective nor the He-Doc spoke. The detective asked me how I felt about the diagnosis, which should have been He-Doc's job. That's all shrinks ever ask, how you feel and shit like that. I began to rock again and I kept my mouth shut. I wasn't about to let them know how I felt.

I rocked for another two hours, long after He-Doc and the detective left my room. And despite the stories the He-Doc had told about me, I began to feel better. I'd just completed the biggest jury case of my life and made a shitload of money for the Innocence Project, and I reminded myself that I had a unique talent that shouldn't go to waste. Earlier that morning, I'd seen a news story on T.V. about a class action lawsuit against the city of Detroit for its lead-lined drinking water pipes that caused cancer in thousands of children. I knew that most class action cases take at least five years to get to trial, and by then, I'd be 101, but I had it in me to do, and I decided that very night that I wanted to fix that case before I died, because the pictures of the children really got to me. I can't explain it, but those pictures really did get to me.

When the He-Doc called me crazy, I didn't care. I'd been called crazy for most of my life and if balancing the scales of justice is crazy, then call me crazy. The thought of righting another wrong – winning one more case – warmed my body like a shot of good Bourbon. It sprung me from my rocker with the vigor of a young woman about to celebrate her last night on the town before starting her dream job. And it made me do what nobody on the ward expected. I put on a sexy slip, knocked on Hardiplank's door and asked him if the 60-minute man was in the house. The next morning, with rosy cheeks and a smirk of my own, I boarded a train for Detroit to have my way with the justice system one last time.

Jo Ann Hoffman

Waiting to Fly Home

A retro Kate Spade evening bag swings from an elegant shoulder
next to me, contents clear inside the glassy sleeve:
she uses Kleenex   crumples bills   smokes Pall Malls,
the slim red packet tossed willy-nilly into the jumble.

My father smoked Pall Malls (in Ohio we said "Pell Mell")
I collected the foil top of each pack   soaked off the backing
in the bathroom sink   wrapped one on the next
built hard silver balls to bombard my brother

The woman shifts the bag to the other elegant shoulder
the fine wool folds of her dress
behave with perfect cashmere grace.

My father wore a gray felt hat
a narrow black ribbon encircling the crown
a monogrammed leather sweatband on the inside rim
"My good hat" he would say "a Dobbs"
and he wouldn't let us touch it
but I did once   trailed my finger
all the way around its downy brim.

The flight desk announces another delay. Kate Spade sighs
surrenders her seat   swivels expertly on spike heel sandals
toward the martini bar across the terminal, little window bag
swinging.

Dad drank Buckeye beer (he loved everything Ohio)
After work he leaned on the kitchen wall, talking to Mom
Pall Mall in his left hand   Buckeye in his right
I leaned against the scratchy wool of his trousers
cradled by a malty ring of smoke.

I'm behind my fashionista in the boarding line,
her seat across the aisle from mine
I settle down content
in the subtle aura of her smoke.

Lynn Gorski

The City of Sorrow and Shame

September 15, 2020 marks the 57th anniversary of one of the most heinous crimes committed against the African American community in an attempt to slow the pace of desegregation in Birmingham, Alabama.

Birmingham, Alabama 1963. Racial tensions are at an all-time high. A federal court orders schools to integrate. The local Ku Klux Klan (KKK) fights every attempt by the African American community to bring integration to Birmingham. The KKK bombs African American homes, businesses, and churches in retaliation for their attempts to break through the white supremacy barrier. The perpetrators are rarely identified; when identified, they are rarely convicted. During a visit to Birmingham in the spring of 1963, Dr. Martin Luther King, Jr. writes, "Its unjust treatment of Negroes in the courts is a notorious reality; there have been more unsolved bombings of Negro homes and churches in Birmingham than any other city in this nation."

The African American community, in response, escalates their struggle to conquer racism and attain the rights intended by the Constitution for all U.S. citizens. The African American community rallies with civil rights leaders at Birmingham's 16th Street Baptist Church, earmarking it as a prime target for the KKK.

September 15, 1963. It is a typical Sunday morning at the 16th Street Baptist Church. Four excited African American children, Addie Mae Collins, Carole Robertson and Cynthia Wesley, all 14-year-olds, gather with 11-year-old Denise McNair in the basement ladies' lounge to prepare for the 10:30 a.m. Youth Day Church Service. As the girls stand by the window and chat, witnesses see a White man get out of a turquoise and white Chevrolet and plant a box under the steps of the church adjacent to the ladies' lounge.

The four young girls have dreams and aspirations similar to all girls their age. The future holds promise for Denise, Addie, Carole, and Cynthia.

Denise McNair, the youngest, plans to be a pediatrician. Her mother teaches school and her father owns a photo shop. Denise is a Girl Scout. She likes softball. One fall day, she organizes the neighborhood kids and puts on a show to raise money for muscular dystrophy.

Addie Mae Collins is an artist whose forte is portraits. Her father, a janitor, struggles to keep his family financially solvent. To help out, Addie and her sisters sell their mother's handmade aprons and potholders door-to-door after school. She is the peacekeeper among her seven siblings and a powerful pitcher on the softball field.

Carole Robertson, a straight-A student and a bookworm, hopes to teach history. Her mother is a librarian, her father, an elementary school band master. It is no surprise Carole plays clarinet in the school band. Carole belongs to Jack and Jill of America, the Girl Scouts, and the Science Club. She takes ballet and tap lessons. She and friends practice popular dances like the cha-cha on her porch and experiment with the latest hairstyles.

Cynthia Wesley spends much of her time on church activities. She is the first adopted daughter of two teachers and excels in math, reading and band. She also organizes lawn parties where she plays music and amuses her friends with witty stories.

The girls look forward to positive, productive futures, but they also experience the ugliness of bigotry.

At the age of six, while Denise and her father shop at Kress Department Store, he leads her downstairs where there are separate bathrooms for "White" and "Colored" girls. "Colored" is a term used by White people to describe African Americans. Denise sees a lunch counter -- smells burgers and onions on the grill and begs her father to buy her a sandwich. She is irate when her father explains they can't buy a sandwich at the counter because of the color of their skin.

Like other African Americans in Birmingham in 1963, when Addie is thirsty, she must bear the indignity of finding a "Colored" water fountain. She cannot drink from a water fountain that is designated "White."

Carole looks forward to Saturday matinees with her sister. The African American kids cannot sit with the White kids and are restricted to the balcony seats. Carole and her sister lob kernels of popcorn over the balcony at the White kids below.

Cynthia's neighborhood was once a garbage dump. African American families clean it up, build nice homes and move in. The KKK prefers the garbage dump and begins terrorizing the neighborhood to frighten the African American residents into abandoning their homes. The neighborhood is dubbed "Dynamite Hill" because of the many unsolved bombings attributed to the KKK. To protect his family, Cynthia's father patrols the area each night with a group of neighbors.

September 15, 1963, 10:22 a.m. As Addie, Carole, Cynthia and Denise ready themselves for the church service, the box placed under the steps explodes. It rips through the church basement, propelling glass and mortar through the air like a cyclone. A short time later, the lifeless bodies of the four young girls are pulled from the rubble.

September 17, 1963. Carole Robertson is buried.

September 18, 1963. The funeral for Addie Mae Collins, Cynthia Wesley and Denise McNair takes place at the 16th Street Baptist Church. In the Eulogy, Dr. Martin Luther King, Jr. says, "Indeed this tragic event may cause the White South to come to terms with its conscience." Dr. King's prophecy holds true. The nation dubs Birmingham the "City of Sorrow and Shame." The bomb, planted by the KKK to slow the pace of desegregation in Birmingham, has the opposite effect, becoming a pivotal point in the struggle. The moderate White community can no longer remain silent. Birmingham's ineptitude for protecting its children outrages the nation and helps ensure the passage of the 1964 Civil Rights Act.

But the road to justice is slow, even though the Federal Bureau of Investigation's (FBI) initial investigation produces evidence against KKK members and witnesses report having seen Robert Chambliss (Dynamite Bob), an active KKK member, near the church that morning.

September 30, 1963, 15 days after the bombing. Chambliss is arrested for possession of dynamite, fined $1,000 and given a six-month jail sentence, which is suspended.

1977, 14 years after the bombing. At long last, Chambliss is charged and convicted of first-degree murder and is sentenced to life in prison. He died in prison 8 years later.

1994, 31 years after the bombing. Suspect Herman Cast dies before being charged.

2001, 38 years after the bombing. Thomas Blanton, Jr. is charged and convicted of the murders. He is sentenced to life in prison.

2002, 39 years after the bombing. Bobby Frank Cherry is charged and convicted of the murders. He is sentenced to life in prison.

Had the girls survived the bombing, they would be in their late 70's today. Denise McNair may have become a pediatrician or found a cure for muscular dystrophy. Addie Mae Collins may have become a diplomat and negotiated peace within the Middle East. Carole Robertson may have become a history teacher and influenced the lives of children. Cynthia Wesley may have become a minister and followed in the footsteps of Dr. Martin Luther King, Jr.

We will never know what the world lost that day, when it lost these four young girls. But what we do know is this: When bigotry rears its ugly head, all of us lose.

Les Brown

The Wish

I never had a birthday party
        but Rickey did.
and I was invited. I went
        down the paved road to his house,
a bigger house than ours.
        I took him a dancing man
daddy made from wood scraps
        he had brought from the factory.

Rickey's house had a bathroom,
        and it was inside
and had a hot water spigot.
        We had a Brownie camera,
but Rickey had a movie projector
        that showed real movies
on a sheet his momma hung
        from the fireplace mantle.

He showed us an Abbot and Costello movie.
        It was funny, especially Costello.
Then we had the fancy cake
        with seven colored candles on it.
Rickey made a wish
        and blew out all of the candles.
I secretly made a wish too.

Elizabeth Kirschner

A Sorry Scheme of Things

Between nothing and nothing, there is this – me, at seventeen, tunnel-vision drunk, swerving my father's station wagon home at 3:00 a.m. Two-lane road, all curves and dips – dark woods, a stream, a patchy acre of jewelweed and grass.

I don't see the deer until it turns its head – road full of eyeballs, small moons glowing. I crank the wheel, stamp both feet on the brake, skid and jolt into the ditch.

Glitter and crunch of broken glass in my lap, deer hair drifting like dust. My chin and shirt are soaked – one eye half-obscured by the cocked bridge of broken glasses on my nose.

With the car still running, its lights angle up at the trees as I get out. The doe lies on its side.

I want to fix the beautiful body, color of wet straw, of oak leaves in winter, but here's what I do: pick the deer up like a bride, wrestle it into the back of the car – the seat folded down.

Somehow, I steer the station wagon out of the ditch and head home, night rushing in through the broken window, headlight dangling, side-mirror gone.

My head throbs, something stabs my side. The deer breathes behind me, shallow and fast.

A stoplight and I'm almost home when the doe scrambles, its long head like a ghost in the rearview mirror. It bites me, teeth clamping down on my shoulder. I scream, struggle and flail until the deer, exhausted, lets go and lies down.

A wonder how my own body, empty, clean of secrets, knows how to drag the deer out of the car, onto the driveway. Shaking, I pat it down, frisk it, like a fish slipped out of its net.

The deer shudders, bleats, its tail a fused filament. By now the doe's eyes are hot tar and my shirt's smelly as dirt.

This is when I know I'll never get to see it: a bright future, never coming close, never dazzling. Clutching the doe, I slap it, scream, *Say it doesn't matter. Say this is enough. Say you want this.*

Around the driveway the trees wave, like mute women trying to alert me to an emergency. Roots like jump ropes. Grass cut like a cancer.

When my father comes out, he yells, "What the hell?" The odor has changed, enormous as a storm, as he walks to the toolshed, comes back lugging a concrete block.

Time freezes. The night hemorrhages snow. When he drops the block on the deer's head, I'm a river diverted from its path. And when God doesn't strike, and the sea doesn't overflow, my voice is a kettle of hawks, circling. My head, lowered, sees how death accepts a special kind of silence. I exhale.

Some things stay with me, like dumping the doe deep in the woods, as though I were a gangster.

All my life, the deer. A mouth growing more exposed without air. The spine, a column of clouds. The remains, a brutal cave.

What did I dread? Right then? My father, a dead doornail, coming into my room, his red robe, opening.

Or was it myself, who had danced in a bar full of misfits that night, squash flowers rotting in my hair?

Drunk, weaving, I danced an obscene dance in a stained red dress under the lowered eyes of men. Shuffling into place, the floor boards browned, wilted while a man twirled, dipped me, as if into a vat of hot wax.

I wanted to drink from his sorry scheme of things, touch the spot that bites back and so I did.

Like him, I had a wide, friendly face, yet I smelled his dishpan breath as I swung my ponytail like a filthy tassel.

Next thing I knew, blood on the sullen ground, blood on the stones, blood on the slope and blood on the fist going into me without any pain. Blood on the green torso of the slavering flies.

Blood in thick amber strokes, blood from my right ear, from his ochre nose. Whose blood was this? On the fender, in my shoe, in his breath? *There's blood,* he said.

Blood here, too, down here, I said.

Only blood, blood on his watch, would it dry? On his whitish wedding band. Would it dry?

Blood on his knee, blood on the faithful knee, the one readied for erotic negation. Blood at the age of seventeen. Blood that was mute and autistic and cauterized and smelled of smelted tar.

Was this mine? Blood on the wheel – bronzed, dead, gold and diamond deep. Blood as fast as the car when I hit the deer. The thud was log-thick.

When I got out, her hide was frayed mohair, her petite feet, small as the ace of clubs.

Dragging her into the woods with my father, then standing in front of her body listening to her bones hiss, like pumice stones, this made me want to drown my hands.

The deer entered my dreams, breathed mist into the pine trees, her fawn, a hot package of breath rising up, like a rocket and falling again, like a rocket.

Death is a lack, I suppose, and love even more so. Years later, when I drive home alone, I go back into the woods where a collapsed star bankrupts the moon.

Dark galaxy of faults where the deer was left, like an underwater statue, the woodsy rooms, abstract.

What I make of the earth is inferred and the undersides of the leaves on the forest floor are a rundown palace, the color, eel-black.

Who I am and was before the deer and the man and my father, when only the stars and only the sea and only the light gushed from its unknown source, this can be charted as precisely as a fever, even though it's absolutely colorless and missing a thingness.

My hands, the ones I wanted to drown, these smell like smelt, as I stand, a condemned building, while the hour, forever it seems, half-steps its crippled way elsewhere.

Susan Alff

Religious Education

…starting with Sunday
shushes shushes along the sides
dips a short swoop across the toe
its book-shaped sponge guiding the milk of the polish
onto young shoes

…once was the early uprising
in the living room   its carpet rife with boxes
the high holy ruckus of brothers in bathrobes ripping
into Christmas

…is not that sleeveless yellow dress covered in eyelet
ruffles scratchy at the armholes and the neck
worn with white gloves and Mary Janes
no

…is it faith hope and clarity   the Golden Rule
the Ten Commandments   five easy ways to bring light
into a small soul

…might be Wednesdays
church school a trailer on the outskirts
of the playground   the sand and bathrobe world
of Jesus rolled up tight
in a wall map

(…but what about the offering
lightened to three pennies
the church dime spent
on ice cream)

what is it that lasts for the end   all facts forgiven
what is left
Child

…comes to this
those New England Saturdays
and our task   transform the room from Grange Hall
to Sunday School   clack open the wood-slat chairs
into rows   thump a hymnal on each   find
candles   crayons   glitter   old magazines
finished   touch a simple chord
on the piano   to fall
into the hush:

let the party begin.

Jesus wept.

That yellow sleeveless dress covered in eyelet, scratchy ruffles at he armholes and the neck
white gloves

The Golden Rule, the Ten Commandments, the Seven Deadly Sins,
5 easy ways to bring light into a small soul

All is well.

What lasts for the end? All the facts forgotten, what is left?

Carols in those soaring boy soprano voices, "What can I give him, poor as I am …
What can I give him, give my heart.
(If I were a shepherd, I would give a lamb.
If I were a wise man, I would do my part.)

fetched up
newfound in New England / our lonely task

Religious Education

Once was,

Now is

Is not

On second thought

Is it?

Might be

What about

Perhaps

Marjorie Schratz McNamara

Discretions

My son tells me he is teaching a class in discrete math
and my mind spills with whispers of false weigh-ins
and the rounding down of dress sizes. He spells it for me:
e-t-e, a math of individual things rather than
continuous lines and figures which heave off
into space. In discrete math, there is exactness, recorded pinpoints,
when counting not measuring is key.

I think of home and sudden guests for dinner
when Mother would signal us an FHB alert--
Family Hold Back—most often on mashed potatoes;
that bowl passed hand to hand along the nine
of us and company, a victory for recorded
pinpoints and potatoes enough
to go around.

Nancy Young

Legacy

Years ago, a decent woman would appear in print only three times: birth, marriage, and death. A 1914 announcement of Amanda Lueck's wedding touted it as one of the "brilliant society events of the season." The gushing newspaper write-up covered several pages. When H.A. Kroner took a wife, people paid attention.

I never met my grandmother, know her only from family lore, her honeymoon journal, a few photos, and that single newspaper clipping.

She was "charming in a gown of ivory white charmeuse with silk shadow lace," shrouded by a veil and carrying bride's roses and lilies of the valley. Beneath the surface fabric, her undergarments were likely plain and mended. Perhaps the cotton chafed against the silk, reminding her of the contrast. When she walked down the aisle, Amanda crossed from a workaday world to one of privilege.

That privilege was on full display. The article preserves attendants' and attendees' gowns in meticulous textile detail: shell pink satin striped taffeta, blue charmeuse, white voile lace, cream point de sprit, and pale green meteor crepe—a galaxy of fashion.

The Wisconsin air must have been heavy with scent. Roses and marguerites, palms and ferns festooned the German Lutheran church, and profusions of yet more roses, carnations and smilax, decorated the reception at the Kroner mansion.

Amanda Ottilia Lueck knew she'd ventured out of place. Twenty years younger than her groom and sensitive about it, she scribbled her worries in her journal with a shaky hand. After a grueling, migraine-inducing train ride, the honeymoon couple checked into the Hotel La Salle in Chicago. She cringed when the hotel clerk "took a good look" at her as her new husband registered them as Mr. and Mrs. The hotel manager watched too. Noting the "just married" label on the couple's trunk, he sent congratulations and carnations.

"Don't watch us," she scrawled in her journal that night. And yet I do watch her, watch them, from a century away.

Her new husband took the liberty of writing in her journal, recording bills paid, bank appointments arranged, art viewed in a gallery, and the fact that "Amanda slept."

I have a picture of her, taken the day H.A. proposed. She's slight, with fine, wavy hair pulled back from her doll-like face. Several tendrils escape to frame her cheeks. She's dressed simply in a white buttoned blouse and long black skirt. Nearly overpowered by a heavy crystal vase full of roses, she rests its weight on a garden bench. Behind her, a fence and a dark Italianate brick house—the Kroner mansion—block out the rest of the landscape. Amanda's eyes stare directly in the camera eye. She doesn't smile.

I think of the heaviness of crystal, how it glitters, how hard it is, how easily it shatters. Amanda struggled to grasp her new role as a rich man's wife. A hardware mogul, H.A. Kroner possessed a ruling hand of galvanized steel. Amanda's hands were small, like mine. Her powers lay in persistence and subterfuge.

Far more at home in the kitchen than in the parlor, Amanda counted the help among her friends. "She'd sit at the kitchen table with the cook, have tea and laugh," my aunt recalled. "They'd talk for hours." Amanda kept her ears open to what went on in the community. "She was sneaky," my mother said. "Made sure her name wasn't attached to the things she did." What good she could do, she managed in secret, funding school field trips, feeding drifters who'd marked her fencepost with the "kindhearted lady" symbol, surreptitiously sending groceries and clothes to those who otherwise would do without.

My mother and aunt confirm that Amanda Kroner remained a gentle force in a rigid household. Though they worshiped her, they concede she wasn't perfect. She couldn't spell. She was guilty of some of the prejudices typical of her era. And she wouldn't openly cross her husband. But in a period when women had no vote, Amanda circumvented barriers. Her voice was muffled, but her actions spoke.

My grandmother's picture sits in my North Carolina living room next to my wedding photo. I wonder what she'd think of me, of my activism, of my stint as a reporter. And I wonder what she would make of her great-granddaughter, whose fists smash glass ceilings.

Janet Joyner

Cook's Feet

Just the feet, in repose, finally.
Right foot on bottom, heels
like worn leather, calloused.
Thin black leg, one ankle
showing, her dress hem
tucked behind the knee
on a hand-hewn wooden
stool. Fingers still busy
at beans, bowl in the lap,
snuff on her bosom, smelling
high. Nor she nor I
ever could seem to get
all the way to comfortable
in that southern house.

Susan Alff

School

Spring, the park's stocked pond is silver-ribboned
with fish—larger than minnows, common as sparrows
—as tightly packed as gumballs in a glass machine.
The dock teems with children, scabby knees
and grievance: whose turn it is to hold the pole
and how to cast and how you scared away my fish
with your loud voice. Mom steps up mid-
complaint to us. "My little mosquitoes."

She takes the pole from us, stands easy on the dock.
Her rod curtsies as she sets the hook
in one smooth flick. Up swings
the weighted line, a fish,
a real fish, struggling on the planks.
The attendant clubs it once.

We too are stunned.

Mom caught a fish, the only one this day.
Her trophy wrapped, she puts it in her tote
and steps back into attendance on us,
the holder of jackets, the purveyor
of sunscreen.

How did she rise from that remembered photo:
standing tall at 12, her name still Shirley,
cuffed jeans above white socks and saddle shoes,
easy on the dock, rod in hand.

She fished before we were the world:
where did she go?

Andrew Birkestrand

Teddy Bears and Sharks

The meeting was held in the board and brick farmhouse a mile outside of town. Three were in attendance. Cynthia the eldest, at sixteen and a half and her little brothers Avery and Dell. Cynthia called the meeting to order, she initiated all their meetings and, her little brothers always came when called. The meeting ritual was observed as it was always observed before summits where profound subject matter would be discussed. Gravely looking into their eyes she locked pinky fingers with each and made them wish for a painful death involving fire ants and underpants should they ever breathe a word about what was about to take place. That rite observed she took her place on top of the three steps that led up from the living room and into the dining room. This architectural quirk created a ready stage for pontification. She stood there in penny-rolled, stone-washed jeans, and a green blouse. Her dirty blond bangs ignored gravity in their freeze-sprayed pursuit of the ceiling.

Avery and Dell sat cross-legged on the green shag carpet of the living room floor. They looked up in rapt attention. Avery, the elder of the two brothers, was supposed to be the last and youngest child in the family. But an oversight made on their parent's date night ushered Dell into the fold fourteen months later. This resulted in their mother going to work as soon as Dell was done breastfeeding. An inconvenient beginning, but one they grew accustomed to quickly.

The brothers were eight and seven and held their older sister in an esteem that only innocence could muster. This was to their benefit because in a house run by Cynthia things occurred her way or not at all at least until their parents came home from work at night.

"Here are the rules," Cynthia said. "First, never use them on me. Understood?"

The boys chirped an affirmative.

"Use them too much and you sound like a moron. Some combos are okay, but others make you sound stupid," She paused. "If Mom and Dad hear you say these things, you'll eat soap, and I'll deny we ever had this conversation. Clear?"

They nodded.

"Good. You'll be moving up at school and the old standbys won't work anymore. So, if I hear you call someone a doody face or poo head again, I'll slap a diaper on you and shut you up with a pacifier. Those are baby words, and you are no longer babies." She paused and stared at Dell. Avery elbowed him, and he extracted his index finger from his nose and wiped it on his shirt.

Cynthia pushed on. "*Stupid*, *hell*, *idiot*, *damn*, and *moron* are still acceptable, but they are the Teddy Bears of the swearing kingdom. You need sharks. I'm referring to terms like *dick*, *cock*, *shit*, *shithead*, and *asshole*. I'm talking about *twat*, *Jesus Christ*, *goddamn*, and *fuck*." She went on, and as she did Avery's blue eyes widened and his jaw dropped under the breadth and scope of her lexicon.

"Wait!" Avery said raising his hand and interrupting the colorful and varied language that rained down on them. He did this because one term she threw was completely foreign to him. What's a *douchebag*?"

"Questions will be addressed at the end of the lesson," she said.

Avery put his hand back down.

"Use the f-word only at special times. Like when you shoot your eye out with a BB gun, or when Mom and Dad run over the cat. It's precious. Don't spend it frivolously. If you really want to let someone have it, add one or two of the Teddy-Bear terms to one of the sharkish ones like, *stupid*, *moronic butt-head*, or *piss-sucking sack-o-shit*. If used correctly, these can be surprising, funny and useful. Some of my personal favorites are: *cock hungry thunder cunt*, *shoe fucking shit bird*, and *twat tasting queef quaffer*."

"Queef cougher?" asked Avery.

"Queef is a girl fart, and quaff means to drink," said Cynthia.

"Eeew; I thought you told us girls don't fart," said Dell who was having trouble holding his head up under the weight of all this information.

"That's right, we don't. Which is why that last string is especially offensive."

"If you want an ear burner, then add *goddamn* to any of these. But if you do," she said, holding up a hand, "you risk eternal hell. So be sure to pray for forgiveness later and bring it up in confession." She made the sign of the cross over her chest before giving them more examples.

"Now, I want each of you to try some out, play with them, and decide which ones work best. You go first," she said, looking at Avery.

The pink tip of Avery's tongue poked out the corner of his mouth. Finally, turning toward his little brother and not wanting to overreach, he ventured, "Little bastard."

"Solid," Cynthia said.

"What's a bastard?" Dell asked.

"It's someone who was born without a father married to their mother," she said.

"But I have a father and he is married to Mom. Isn't he?" he asked.

"Yes, he is, but when swearing it can also mean a very bad person," Cynthia said.

"What kind of bad person?"

"The kind that eats all the Frosted Flakes and drops ninja farts in the car," said Avery. Dell slugged him in the arm.

"Ninja farts?" asked Cynthia.

"Silent but deadly," said Dell grinning.

"Well, we're all learning today, aren't we?" she said.

"What's *bitch* mean?" Avery asked.

"That has several different meanings depending on who says it and how it's used. The real meaning is a female dog. But…"

"Wait, wait. Let me get this straight. Nellie is a bitch?" Avery asked, looking out the sliding glass door to the dog laying in the house thrown shade on the cement patio. It was the black lab's favorite spot to lay down on hot spring days.

"Yes, she is," said Cynthia who descended the steps and tapped on the sliding glass door that led to the patio. "and she's just the sweetest bitch there is too. Aren't you Nellie?" she said in an overly precious tone. Nellie regarded Cynthia through the window with weary brown eyes and then rested her head on her paws. Cynthia returned to her perch and continued.

"But *bitch* can also mean to complain a lot, or it can refer to a mean girl. Oddly, it can also be used to indicate something is awesome."

"How do you use it to mean that?" asked Dell.

"If someone tells you something good, something you like, instead of saying good, cool, or awesome. Just say *bitchin.* For example, *I am one bitchin' sister.*"

"So, bitch is for girls and bastard is for boys?" Dell asked.

"Yes, but bitch can be used for a boy too if you want to offend his boy-ness."

"Bitchin," said Avery.

"But you never, and I repeat never, call a girl a cunt," she added.

"Why not?" Dell asked.

"Well, one day you may want to have a girlfriend, and no girl would waste time on an asshole who calls a girl a cunt. It's ugly and unforgivable."

"What if we don't want girlfriends?" asked Dell.

"Then you won't say it for the simple reason that I'll kick your ass if you do." she said. The hall clock's pendulum swung, and the hands on its yellowed face ticked loudly in the silence as the little brothers considered her words. Finally, Avery flicked Dell's ear.

"Son of a bitch," Dell said, rubbing his earlobe.

"She's your mom too asshole," Avery said.

They both grinned.

Cynthia looked at her Swatch. "I think that's enough of a lesson for now. I have a friend coming over to study, and we'll need privacy, so go upstairs and practice quietly."

"Who's the friend?" Dell asked.

"Just someone from school."

"Is it the Toilet Boy?" Avery asked. One of Avery and Dell's favorite hobbies was listening in on their sister's phone conversations. She spent hours on the phone with her friends from school, and the brothers found such surveillance both educational and entertaining. Lately, the name Hanover had been brought up many times; often in conjunction with declarations of adoration. The boys found these hilarious. Swooning's of "he's so sweet and hot and I just want to lick him up and down," never failed to crack them up. This was due to the boy's name, Hanover Crane. It was, coincidentally, also the name of the manufacturer of the upstairs toilet. The name stenciled in blue paint on the top of the back rim of the porcelain bowl.

"Never mind who. The only concern you two have is staying in your room and leaving us alone."

The doorbell rang. "There he is," she said, checking herself in the living room mirror.

"Is he your boyfriend?" asked Dell.

"Do Mom and Dad know you have a boy coming over?" asked Avery.

"That's it; If you don't get lost, I'll tell Mom and Dad that I caught you playing on the roof."

"You wouldn't dare," said Avery.

"Try me," she said.

"We don't want to watch you two suck face anyway," Avery said, and the boys reluctantly went upstairs to their room.

On one side of the room were two desks topped with shelves and filled with toys. On the other side sat two twin beds. They were covered by twisted zoo animal jungle sheets. On the far wall opposite the door, the dormer window streamed bright sunlight over the boys' personal kingdom. Dust motes jigged in the light. The room had the slight odor of moldy pizza and dirty underwear. This was due to Dell smuggling a piece of pizza up to his room a week ago. After half-finishing it, Dell dropped it to molder underneath his bed. The floor was strewn with stuffed animals and with discarded clothes that would take their time finding their way into the hamper. Here they practiced their new vocabulary, but their swear-a-thon ended when they heard Cynthia and her guest pound up the steps and slam the door to her room.

"She's not supposed to have boys in her room," said Dell. "Mom said so."

Avery held a finger to his lips, shushing his brother. He lay down on the floor next to the grate underneath Dell's desk and listened. Dell joined him. It connected their room to the vent in their sister's room. If they were quiet, they could sometimes hear conversations or music. Such methods were often necessary to keep abreast of family activity. After a while Dell whispered, "Do you hear anything?"

Avery shushed him and wiggled closer to the grate. "It's definitely a boy's voice."

"What's he saying?" asked Dell.

"I think I heard *God*."

"They're praying?" asked Dell.

"Oh, oh, *fuck*. I definitely heard the word *fuck*," said Avery, excited.

"They're fighting?" asked Dell.

At that moment, a *Yes, yes* issued loud and clear from the grate.

"I don't think so," said Avery. "Maybe they're practicing their swear words, too."

"Cynthia doesn't need any practice," said Dell.

"Practice makes perfect."

"What's that squeaking?" asked Dell.

"I think it's the bed. Maybe they're jumping up and down on it."

"Bitchin'," said Dell, who rose from the floor, climbed onto his own bed, and started jumping. Avery got up and started working the springs of his own bed. They were having so much fun they didn't even hear Cynthia's guest leave.

Swearing became a favorite pastime for the boys, but their enthusiasm often outran their skill. Before praying and climbing into his bed at night, Dell would stretch and say, "Goddamn twat waffles, I'm tired." Avery would respond by falling into his bunk and yawning "mmm *waffles"* in return.

At St. Thomas school, when Avery's teacher Sister Anne and the other nuns were out of earshot, they met up at recess to mesmerize their classmates with new and inventive swearing exhibitions. They dropped the words *shit*, *bitch*, *dick*, and even an occasional *goddamn* at these times to the amazement and admiration of their peers. The sheer shock and awe of using the words at school was a joy. During one demonstration Avery called Dell's teacher Sister Anne "a frigid fucking whore for God."

And Dell who was a little sweet on his teacher responded with, "Watch your mouth. You inbred Nazi horse cock." The crowd of classmates about them fell slack jawed and silent under the brothers obvious skill.

Perhaps they became too comfortable. One day when the boys were helping their dad bring the groceries in from the garage;

Avery's foul language got the better of him. The bag Avery carried in was wet from the rain and tore before he reached the house. An entire eight pack of green glass Mountain Dew bottles dropped to the floor. The crash and splash of glass and pee-green soft drink broke around his feet and a "*Fucken shit*", sprang from his mouth. All of this occurred in the presence of his father who at that moment stepped up behind him.

A second later, the ground disappeared as he was snatched up out of his shoes and into the air. Avery, now tucked under his father's arm, got a glimpse of Dell who mouthed the words *oh shit* and waved as Avery was borne away. He was carted all the way through the kitchen and house to the bathroom. There a bar of wet soap waited. His father grabbed the soap and energetically went to work. Periodically, he pelted his son with questions.

"What did you just say?"

The taste of sharp, oily, cringe-worthy bitterness filled Avery's mouth and swamped his taste buds as his father sawed the bar back and forth across teeth and tongue.

"Where did you hear that word? Where? Who have you heard talking like that?"

Avery didn't know how to answer with a mouthful of soap. This may have occurred to his father too because he paused scrubbing and extracted the bar.

"Athsthchool," Avery spat through tears and Dial-coated teeth.

"Well, Sister Anne's gonna hear about this." He dropped the remains of the bar into the sink with a "tunk" before stomping off to clean the garage. Avery wasn't sure, but he thought he heard his father mumble, "Goddamn, what kind of bullshit are they teaching at that school?" as he left.

Avery spit soap flakes into the sink, and tried to rinse the oily perfumed substance from his mouth. He kept hissing *fuck* as if the power of that word would strip the taste of soap from his tongue. When he finally came up for air, he felt someone watching him from the doorway. Cynthia stood there, smirking and shaking her head.

"Warned you potty-mouth," she said.

The boys didn't see much of Cynthia the next few weeks. She was busy with the Toilet Boy, who would come over occasionally and disappear with her into her room. They had spied on him through their bedroom window as he parked his red pickup in the driveway and strutted up to the house. He often wore acid-washed blue jeans, high tops, and a t-shirt, and he always had sunglasses covering his eyes or perched on his head.

"He doesn't look so special," said Avery.

"Yeah, look at his hair," said Dell. It was red, spikey, and cut short in the front and left long in the back.

"He looks like a rooster," said Avery.

Rooster or not he was around so much that the boys had taken to calling him TB as it was less of a mouthful than The Toilet Boy honorific.

One late June afternoon, they were riding bikes in the gravel drive when TB's red truck barreled down their road. The handlebars had loosened on Avery's bike and wouldn't hold the fork of his front tire stable. He was holding the tire with his legs and muscling the handlebars back on straight when TB pulled up next to him.

"Having some bike trouble?" he asked.

Avery nodded, and TB got out of the truck. "You must be Avery?"

"And that's Dell," Avery said as the littler boy pedaled up to them.

"I'm Hanover. I'm a friend of your sister's."

"We know," said Dell.

"Well, I think I can fix your bike problem."

Avery handed the bike over to TB and watched as he propped it up next to the truck. Then the older kid reached into the cab of the vehicle and pulled out a small box. Inside it, were several L-shaped bars.

"Come over here and hold the bike still for me," he said. Avery did so.

"The handlebars are loose, so we need to tighten them up. See here?" he pointed to a bolt just behind the handlebars in the direction of the seat. "That's the Allen bolt."

Avery nodded.

"Know what these are?" He held up the little tools.

"Allen wrenches," Avery said.

"Yeah, they are. How did you know that?"

"My dad used them when he put the bike together," said Avery.

"Duhhhh," said Dell a few feet away.

The Toilet Boy laughed. "Well, we'll use them again and have you rolling in no time."

To Avery's surprise, a few twists of the wrench and his bike's handlebars were back on straight. Hanover then strode up to the house where Cynthia waved from the deck. They disappeared for a couple hours inside the house. Later when the boys were hot and sweaty, they tried to go in for a drink but found the doors locked.

TB soon left, and Dell and Avery watched from their bikes as he pulled away. His visits became more frequent after that and they saw less and less of Cynthia.

At first, Cynthia's preoccupation with TB didn't bother them at all. She was the one who made them do the dishes, pick up their toys, and scrub the toilet. She made sure they didn't eat all the cereal in one sitting or play on the roof. So, a break from her influence didn't bother them. They enjoyed the looser restrictions and lack of accountability. Their parents, however, were another matter.

"Christ! Pick up your damn Legos," Dad said, hopping up and down and holding his foot. "I almost broke my neck!"

"I just bought Mountain Dew yesterday, and today it's all gone," their Mom said, picking up one of several empty bottles they had forgotten on the kitchen counter.

"Jesus, we're not made of money," Dad said. "No more pop if they are going to guzzle it like water."

For Avery and Dell, the price of this freedom and excess revealed itself as the caffeine withdrawal set in.

"I hate TB" moaned Dell. He lay on his bed holding his head as if trying to keep it from splitting.

"That name's too good for him," Avery croaked from under a pillow. "From now on, he's The Shitter."

Another couple of weeks passed without their sister's guiding hand, and they missed her. One night, well after bedtime, Dell padded out in his pajamas and tentatively knocked on her door.

"Cynthia, can I watch the Late Show with you tonight?" he asked. Occasionally, if she was feeling generous, she let him snuggle under the blanket with her and watch *The David Lettermen Show* on her mini black and white television. Not the whole show, of course, just up through the top ten list. It was their thing, and even though he didn't get half the jokes, he enjoyed the time with her.

"Not tonight Dell." she said.

Dell slumped like a sail without wind and dragged himself back to bed.

Avery also missed his sister. Sometimes she would set the VCR to tape the Friday midnight hour of MTV and watch it with him. The last time she'd done this was over a month ago. The only music video that hadn't been watched into static was Peter Gabriel's stop motion monstrosity "Sledgehammer." which gave him nightmares. She had introduced him to "Fight for Your Right to Party" by the Beastie Boys, and he was forever grateful. Hell, he'd even put up with her making him watch "Mandolin Rain" by Bruce Hornsby and the Range again. Once she'd refused to let him leave the room until he watched that video twenty times with her. He had nightmares involving pianos for weeks after viewing it so much, but he'd put up with it again for some time with his sister.

One day in early July she came home in tears. Her makeup was smeared down her face in black and blue streaks as she raced past them up to her bedroom.

They trickled up the stairs after her. They had never seen their sister cry before, and the sight unnerved them. They loitered outside her door for a bit, not sure if they wanted to know what could rattle her so much. Eventually, they knocked.

"Go away!"

She did not come to dinner that night, telling her Mom and Dad she felt ill. Her chair sat empty at the dinner table, and the absence ruined Avery and Dell's appetite. They were used to her making funny faces at them when Mom and Dad weren't looking, which made them splutter food in laughter. There was no laughter during dinner that night; there was just chickpeas, meat loaf, and questions about what they did that day. They ate a full helping's worth of meatloaf, but only because they couldn't leave the table without cleaning their plates. After Mom and Dad had gone to bed, they walked down the hallway to their sister's room. They didn't knock. They just pushed the door open and padded over to where she lay on the bed, her arms covering her face.

"What's wrong?" they asked.

She hugged them both to her. "He's an asshole," she said.

"Fuck him," Dell said, but this just made Cynthia start to cry again.

"I told him I loved him."

"We love you," said Avery. She held them both tighter.

"Cynthia, you're crushing my soul," croaked Dell. But she didn't let go, and the brothers didn't complain again.

Things got back to normal after that. Cynthia monitored the execution of her brothers' chores. She made sure they cleaned their room and she kept them away from candy and sugar. Sometimes, Avery would catch her looking sad but these looks were fleeting. she began to joke more. Things seemed to be getting better. Unfortunately, better in this case meant the boys had to regularly wash the dishes from breakfast and lunch before Mom and Dad got home. This odious activity afforded them a perfect view through the kitchen window. It was through this window and during this chore that the boys saw the red pickup spit gravel down their country road.

"It's The Shitter. He's back!" squeaked Dell.

Dell and Avery watched as Hanover turned in the drive, parked, and climbed out of the truck. They locked the front door and killed the kitchen lights long before he finished climbing the front steps of the deck to knock on the door.

"What do you want?" asked Avery through the door.

"Is that Dell?" asked The Shitter.

"No," said Avery.

"It's me. Han, Hanover Crane. I helped you fix your bike awhile ago, remember?"

"Uh huh," said Avery.

"Look, pal. I came over to see Cynthia. Can you tell her I'm here?"

"Tell him to fuck off," hissed Dell.

"What was that?" The Shitter asked.

"Um have you tried calling her?" Avery asked knowing full well all of his attempts at this were met with slammed receivers and unplugged phone cords.

"Yeah… but I haven't had any luck getting through." he said.

"Is she expecting you?" asked Avery.

"No. it's a surprise. She'll want to talk to me, though."

"I'm sorry Cynthia's not here," said Avery.

"Yeah, piss off!" squeaked Dell.

"Listen, you little shits. I'm here to talk to Cynthia, and you're going to get her for me." He pounded on the door, and the boys flinched back from the blows.

"What's going on?" asked Cynthia. "Who are you two talking to?"

Avery and Dell spun around to find Cynthia standing there in the kitchen, her arms crossed over her chest. She must have heard the pounding all the way up in her room and came down to investigate.

"It's the Shitter," said Avery.

"But it's okay. We told him to piss off," said Dell.

"Who?" she asked.

"Hanover Crane," said Avery.

"Cynthia, is that you?" asked the shitter. "I just came to talk. Can you just open up and let me in?"

"You boys go and play," Cynthia said. Avery and Dell didn't move.

"Go. I got this," she said.

They left the kitchen and ran upstairs to their room. Inside they quietly pried their dormer window up and crawled out onto the roof. They scuttled across the roof as quietly as possible until they came to the part that hung over the deck and front door. There, they stopped and listened to the conversation below.

"Come on, Cynth. Please just let me in."

"Why should I?" Cynthia asked.

"I just want to talk."

"We're talking now."

"Come on, Cynth. We could chat and maybe have a little fun."

"I heard you had fun with that sophmore at McCallister's party last week. Why don't you go talk to her?"

"Cynth, I messed up. I'm sorry. But we were getting so serious, you know? It kind of freaked me out. It didn't mean anything. I'd been drinking. Please forgive me. You know you're the only one for me."

Cynthia didn't say anything for some time, which was too much for Dell. He crawled forward and poked his nose over the gutter to look down at the unwelcome visitor.

"Leave our sister alone you silly asshat," he said.

The Shitter stepped back and looked up, catching a glimpse of Dell before Avery pulled him back and out of sight. "Watch your mouth, you little turd. The grown-ups are talking here."

"What did you just call my brother?" Cynthia asked.

"No offense Cynth, but your little brothers are mouthy little bastards," he said, pushing his sunglasses up on his head. "Let me in, and I'll make it up to you."

"I think not," she said, then she yelled at the ceiling. "Dell, get off the roof now. And Avery, you better not be up there either!"

Avery and Dell both stood up to inch their way back to their bedroom window, but paused to hear the rest of the conversation.

"And you, you cheating sack of shit, piss on you!" she said.

"Cynth, don't be that way. It'll never happen again."

"You bet it won't. Go away."

But he didn't go, no he stood there pounding on the door and pleading and showed no sign he had any intention of leaving until he got what he came for — until two yellow streams arced out over the roof's edge and splattered down on the Shitter's mullet, shoulders, and face. The Shitter spluttered and squealed under the warm yellow liquids. He stumbled back and involuntarily heaved almost losing his lunch and slipped down the stairs of the deck, yelping in pain as his ankle twisted on the way down. He hobbled away swearing at the two little boys who, after pulling their shorts back up, waved and flipped him the bird from the roof. They giggled and watched until the swearing and spitting Shitter wiped the urine out of his eyes, got in his truck and fish-tailed it down the gravel road and out of sight.

Cynthia stepped out onto the deck and looked up at her little brothers, who were still grinning.

"What the hell did you two just do?"

The boys shrugged.

"I think we pissed him off," said Dell.

Glenna D. Wolfe

The Kid

I was thirteen and under age
but someone had to drive
to find you. I'd honk the old Buick
Waaaaah wah-wah, at the houses
of your friends – Jimmy's, Ronny's….
One by one I'd get a wave-off
and go to the next. Every person
in Ozark knew our family signal.
Finally, you'd show, raise your hand
and amble toward the car,
Baby Dog trotting to keep up.

Kirk, it's almost dark! Get in! We're
going to be late for supper. Where
have you been for three hours?
A shrug, a grin and a flush
of freckles, then we were on our
way back across town, Baby Dog
hot and panting between us. You
smelled of licorice and sunshine.

Anne Kissel

Lullaby

At Hancock Shaker Village visitors walk round the round stone barn, marveling at its engineering and construction, wondrous and holy as any pyramid. On quiet spring days the farm comes alive with ghosts of Brothers and Sisters who once worked and worshiped there. They shadow volunteers and staff tending descendant sheep and corn, guardians of their signature weaving and carpentry, the efficient husbandry. If they catch the breeze just so these new keepers of old traditions might hear whispered guidance, a nudge towards inspired perfection from the former residents.

One expects the exquisite craft; most visitors know of the 'classic Shaker' style. That melding of utility and esthetics is displayed everywhere, sharp contrast to modern disposable sensibilities. Each building and its contents, no matter how prosaic the purpose, reflects those hand-wrought values. Tables and chairs hang on walls like artwork, still useful when not in use. The smallest baskets and boxes shine with craftsmanship and eye appeal far beyond what is needed to hold yams or yarn. Everywhere function is wed to beauty, for both were given in praise and all they did, every day, was in praise and joy.

The Meeting Room where men and women came together to sing and move in the spirit echoes with different whispers, their only allowed moments of sensual connection. Visitors with the right angle on time might see the fine overlay of dust shimmer and vibrate with spectral forms, perhaps hear with their deepest ears the trembling, rocking, chanting, singing ecstasy of those long ago sacred hours of sublime and sublimated worship.

In the Infirmary the same faith, its manifestation in beauty and duty, was imbedded into care for the sick and the injured. They knew loveliness and comfort were as healing as potions or medicines. Wooden cradles were made for sick adults, finely crafted as any table in the Village. The cradles sat long and low, inches off the floor, allowing a Sister to rock her ill friend with one foot as she knit and moved in her own finely made chair. The dying need rocking as much as the new born.

True believers, seekers of simplicity and song or perhaps just a safe new family stopped arriving many years ago. The few remaining communities long since ceased recruiting and admitting new members; no more were accepted into that beautiful, impossible, graceful, doomed life. The Smithsonian Magazine reported there are but two Shakers left in the world. Who will rock the last one?

Sandra Dreis

The Old Country

A futile argument carbonates, my brain
feels like the Nehi Grape soda I want,
and my flushed cheeks are the dark sweet
cherries in the brown bag Grandpa tosses.
A pale employee makes the check-out catch.

But Grandpa continues his grocery spiel as I grow
smaller and smaller like a melting popsicle.
Gonifs! Thieves, I'm telling you. Cherries
in ze olt country—zey were three cents a pount.
Three pennies! Go on. Keep your fancy cherries.

I'm thirteen, Flushing, Queens, nineteen sixty-five,
and his loud voice, foreign accent overwhelms.
I need to hide, burrow. Instead, blocked by Grandpa's
large gestures, I smile big and turn my back to blend in
with baseball-card-bubblegum and assorted Lifesavers.

Cash registers clang. A dozen shoppers gather to witness
Grandpa's matinee. Grateful this isn't eight shows a week,
I abandon my unpaid, humiliated bottle of grape soda
and flee, mash the heavy exit door. Pant as if pursued
by evil Russian Tsar Nikolai, himself. I breathe. Safe on Main.

A rerun. I picture the familiar grocery store scenario:
Grandpa slaps down two soggy dollar bills, harvests
coins one-at-a-time from his girly change purse, stalks
out of the A & P clutching one bag—bread, butter and milk.
Tweed sport jacket masks *Mr. Hyde, shopper.* Outside,

stinky busses belch. Doors open. Hiss, mass transit
passing gas. Kerchiefed passengers exit, Grandpa eyes
me on the sidewalk, hands me the bundle, squeaks opens
his rolling metal cart. Ancient. We take up the whole street.
The whole city. The rusty basket wobbles, bumps my ankles.

There's no point in saying what he cannot hear at eighty.
Grandpa's oversize ears hardly work. Besides, he's mine.
So for once, I control my teenage fuse and only *think* it…
Oh Grandpa. This is America. Not—The Old Country.
How I want my grape soda. Those dark sweet cherries.

Rick Forbess

An Unfortunate Rescue

Paul and Gloria left the trail at Blue Jay Stream and in no time were lost in the wilderness, like she planned. Until that moment they had not varied their routine of three decades. Once a year they hiked a thirteen-mile trek along pristine streams, through stretches of old-growth forest, and over ridges offering views of mountains lined up like ragged pyramids. On this occasion Gloria led her husband into a heavily forested tract with steep peaks and narrow valleys whose slopes were covered in rocky outcroppings. She had imagined an experience more picturesque and a hell of a lot safer. That's life. Usually nothing like what one imagines and almost always worse.

Gloria congratulated herself for the reasonably good job of pulling it off. Except for taking cover in the brush to avoid being seen from the air, they started and stopped as pleased. If following a brook or walking a ledge was too difficult or boring, they simply changed course. Only occasional whistles in the distance or someone yelling their names broke the tranquility, so she found periods of serenity. Short-lived, sweet, and unexpected.

She and Paul didn't have real conversations, but when he repeated questions – "Why are my clothes dirty?" "Where are we going?" "Have the girls graduated from high school?" – Gloria answered each time. She was used to it. Once, while they sat on the bank of a small stream, Paul blurted, "Adios, motherfuckers." She loved a cocktail of that name, and it was also dialogue from a short story he had read aloud to her fifteen years earlier. Gloria didn't know which he was referring to and didn't ask. It was amusing, and not unkind to find it so.

After a week of near perfect fall weather, it rained a brief downpour late into the day's hike, and Paul twisted a knee coming down a rocky slope. He winced and let out a high-pitched yelp.

Gloria cursed out loud for not being more careful about the path she chose. Paul deserves better.

"You okay, Gloria? You okay?"

Where did that come from? It was the first time in weeks he addressed her by name.

"I'm fine, sweetie, but your knee must really hurt."

"It does. What did I do?"

Gloria decided to find a place to settle in. Surely the search had been called off or at least dialed back, and the despair in Paul's eyes rattled her. Enough was enough. Time to gather herself for what was coming.

She sat Paul under a pine tree and squatted down to make eye contact.

"Paul, look at me. Now pay attention. This is important. I'm going to find us a place that's dry to spend the night. You stay right here. Don't move. I won't be gone long, okay?"

"Are we going home now?"

"Not now, honey, but later. Just wait here for me."

Her forced smile passed without comment. During most of their long marriage this would not have been the case. Something direct and hard, maybe "Don't pull that bullshit on me" or "You're lying your ass off again" would have been more like it. Better than Paul's god-awful, blank stare. Well, that's not really true. He was always so persistent about getting to the truth of the matter, about honesty; noble in theory but harmful in this instance.

Gloria brushed strands of Paul's gray hair from his face and kissed both cheeks before leaving him. He pulled away and stared into the thick undergrowth. She touched his cheek and walked away without glancing back.

Within a few minutes, Gloria found a shallow depression stretching several feet under a car-sized boulder and switched her headlamp on for an inspection. The space was roomy enough, and there were no signs of critters, so it would do. Safe harbor in a tangled corner of the wilderness. End of the line.

She hurried back to find Paul still under the pine tree, bent over rubbing his knee. He seemed mildly surprised to see her.

"Where have you been? I hurt my knee."

"I know, sweetie. That's why we're stopping for a while. You need to get off that knee and rest. I found a perfect spot."

She helped Paul straighten and lifted his arm over her shoulder for support like he used to do for her after the department-wide holiday parties. "Chemists should know better," she heard him say a thousand times. He didn't lecture, though, and always called the offended parties the next morning to apologize for Gloria's behavior, but so many bridges had been torched over the years. Former friends who were living and half-way functional got their fill long ago, except for the Donikas. They were so smug about their perfect children and preachy about everything else that Gloria had done the shunning for once.

They moved in tandem over the uneven terrain, Paul wincing with each step, and Gloria reassuring him they were almost there. They reached the outcropping in fading light, and a cold northwest wind chilled their faces. She felt exhausted, at the end of her rope, and knew Paul must be also. To top it off, they had no more water and only a few dried apple slices.

"There it is, Paul. Let's get warm and comfy. You'll have to crawl, but I'll help you in, okay?"

"No."

"Come on now, honey. We could snuggle. Wouldn't that be nice?"

Paul didn't answer but yielded to Gloria's nudge to the dark opening, and at her insistence, inched his way in on hands and knees. She followed, dragging her backpack over the litter of old leaves and pebbles.

Gloria removed Paul's boots and set them next to hers in a corner before pulling the attached sleeping bags up to their chins.

The sound Paul made when he tried to wiggle out reminded Gloria of a cat mewing. When she rolled on top of him and pinned his shoulders for a few seconds, he settled down. How odd to be the one in charge, the strong one. She still loved him, or at least she loved the man he was seven or eight years ago. That's the man she thought of as she held him flat on his back.

"Relax, relax. Let's rest in here for a while. Wait for the weather to get better. Remember that hike in the Wind Rivers? How the wind howled? We were snug and warm in our little tent. This is like that."

She knew it was nothing of the sort, but when Paul seemed to glimpse a happy memory, he calmed, and she needed that from him. He had to cooperate now, to work with her. Returning to their home was out of the question. How could they? The days when Paul could be depended on to manage everything were long gone. Even cleaning himself after using the bathroom was a challenge now. And the girls? What a joke. They were off into the wild blue yonder, one with a career "at the intersection of IT and interior house paint selection", and the other trailed by a long line of good-for-nothing tom cats from one Comic-Con convention to another.

Gloria switched her headlamp on and tried coaxing Paul to sing Beatle songs he used to love. The tactic often worked at home, but several minutes passed before he stilled. Gloria listened to his breathing. Its steady rhythm signaled sleep.

She pulled an envelope, labeled "Too Our Daughters", from the pocket of her down vest. It contained a family picture from 2004 with a note on the back Gloria had written weeks earlier.

Dear Rosalyn and Annie,

First of all, I want you to know that your father and I love you both and tried our best to be the parents you deserve, and I suppose you tried to be the children we deserve. Secondly, I love your father, and I know he has always loved me. Over the last several months life for us has become intolerable, however, and I've decided to release us. I hope you will forgive me for what I've done and understand this act of mercy and grace.

Love,

Mom

The smiling faces in the photograph seemed terribly naïve, but how could they have known? They were all healthy back then. Careers were in full swing. Paul was on sabbatical, hoping to finish his fourth novel, and Gloria's drinking hadn't cost her a job yet. The girls were making some bad choices but nothing out of the ordinary for teenagers. Gloria expected that in time they would return to a respectful appreciation for their parents, but the gap between their lives had only widened.

A few weeks earlier she talked to the girls separately and hung up both times with a sharpened awareness of how alone she was. Clearly, Rosalyn's latest promotion and Annie's trip to Burning Man were the reasons for their calling, not concern for her or Paul. Something he used to quote comparing a serpent's sharp tooth to ungrateful children came to mind.

Gloria slid the envelope into the side pocket of the backpack and pulled out a metal flask. When she raised on an elbow to take a long draw, Paul shifted slightly but did not wake.

If they were eventually found, she imagined their daughters using words like tragic, courageous, loving devotion, or even noble. This would be the preferred slant of the newspaper articles. Please, no pictures of ragged clothing drooping over decomposed remains, but a wide angle of the lumpy sleeping bags would be reasonable.

God, how morbid, but better than watching Paul waste away to a dry husk in a nursing home. Better than a drunk wife's half-ass attempts to stave off losing everything, or had it been lost already? Waking up hung over and fully clothed on the couch to find Paul standing naked on the back porch was bad enough once, but twice in the same week was beyond the pale. Bills were unpaid, medical appointments skipped, and housekeeping all but abandoned.

The whiskey and trapped body heat comforted Gloria. She took her time emptying the flask, and her confidence grew. It was time to act. At the bottom of the backpack was a loaded Glock 19 wrapped in a hand towel. Gloria had fired the pistol once before, at the range the day she bought it, so she knew it would be loud and deadly. Fumbling to pull the gun out and unwrap it, she told herself to act quickly, without hesitation. First Paul, then herself. End of story.

Gloria lay in the ambient twilight listening to the wind blow through the tree tops, surprised that she had fallen asleep. The headache and dry mouth were familiar though, so she knew to lie still with her eyes closed.

Had it really happened? Did she point the pistol an inch from Paul's temple, turn her face away, and squeeze the trigger? Yes, but some idiot had left the safety on. Shoving the barrel into her own mouth was no more than dramatic posing, but counting backwards from ten before tossing the gun at four took the cake. The sound of the pistol clanking on a boulder and bouncing into a stand of low bushes meant one sure thing. She would die of dehydration. She knew what to expect from online descriptions. An ugly progression, one that would not end without suffering and regret.

That she was alone in the sleeping bag was unexpected, but Gloria had neither the energy nor the will to move or call out. Paul's hooded coat lay just outside the entrance, and a bit further his pants and underwear. Gloria figured he was closer to the end than she, so his ordeal would be less painful. Now it was only a matter of enduring, waiting for the end.

Judging by the sun's angle, it must have been early afternoon when the dog appeared. Gloria had been drifting in and out of sleep since early morning and was trying to make sense of a blurry dream when a yellow lab's barks and whines jolted her fully awake. She understood right away that she had been found. There would be questions and shame. What else she couldn't imagine, only that it would be awful. Within seconds she heard the voices, a man and a woman shouting her and Paul's names. Gloria watched the man gather Paul's clothing, and the woman crawl in beside her.

After a quick assessment of Gloria's medical status, the woman reassured Gloria that she would be okay and that Paul would be too.

"He's in pretty rough shape, but he's in good hands now, so don't worry."

"Where is he?"

"He's bundled up nice and warm and on his way to the ambulance already."

"How did you find me?"

"Shortbread just followed your husband's scent back to you."

During the nearly three-hour extraction, the rescuers said little and asked fewer questions than Gloria had feared.

Now what? Nursing home? Homeless? Prison? She no longer had a headache, and the water and granola bar had lifted her spirits somewhat. She considered that maybe there's a guiding hand in life, that the wretched affair might lead her to some connection to a life worth living, but probably not.

Lights from several warden service and volunteer vehicles were parked in a rough semi-circle at the trailhead. Their inward pointing beams of light reminded Gloria of the scene from "First Encounters of the Third Kind". An ambulance was parked in the center of the ring of lights. The steady hum of its engine was occasionally broken by a brisk question or statement from one of the people standing around a stretcher.

Oh, dear god, a television crew. Gloria recognized the young reporter from channel eight, the one with a perfect complexion who covered the fires, car wrecks, and shootings. Her cameraman stood to her side, capturing the interview with two young women. The shorter of the two glanced Gloria's way and raised both hands to cover her mouth. Gloria recognized Annie, skinnier and deeply tanned, but her without a doubt, and Rosalyn the woman next to her.

They broke away and ran to Gloria's side calling out to her. Annie stroked their mother's head and bent down to whisper in her ear. "It's okay, Mom. You're safe now."

Rosalyn held her hand and repeated "I love you. I love you."

The girls' jumbled reassurances to help their parents' settle into the best possible life, washed over Gloria. She raised on her elbows to kiss her daughters' cheeks and to be engulfed in their embrace.

When the doctor tapped Rosalyn's shoulder and asked to speak with her and Annie for a moment, Gloria relaxed and wept. It was a miracle. They were a family again.

When the girls turned back to Gloria, they were crying too. One of the rescuers stepped forward holding an envelope.

"You're Rosalyn and Annie, right?"

"Yes."

"I'm so sorry about your father, but this is for you. We found it in your mother's pack."

Sandra Dreis

Aunt Nellie

Petite Aunt Nellie defines *pretty*. Its surface,
allure, two dimensions made three. The how of it.
I'm twelve. I want her secrets. She's brunette,
dark sparkly eyes. Melamine skin, no visible pores,

unlike mom, efficient no-frills schoolteacher
always minus makeup—well maybe just lipstick.
Basic buttoned-up style. Permanent press,
no-iron top to bottom. Hair, Aqua Net finish.

I need a guided tour of Nellie's walk-in closet:
assorted wigs on styrofoam, stacked hat boxes,
satin makeup bag filled with tubes and potions.
Perfume atomizers, delicate colored bottles,

every shape. My aunt catches me squinting,
grading my face, magnifying mirror a monster.
Unforgiving. Forgettable chin, light eyelashes,
pale brows, oversize ears, chandelier lobes

and frizzy hair that hides them. Substantial
nose, a bit too wide. Nellie, my advisor,
gives me the go-ahead. Suggests makeup.
Oh. My self-regard circles the drain. She's hinting…

I'm kind of plain. Nellie directs my makeover,
beauty wizard, wand in hand: liquid eyeliner,
turquoise shadow, brow highlights, blackest
mascara. Pressed powder subdues shine,

rose lipstick accents pursed lips. Coral blush.
Cheekbones emerge, big striking eyes.
Magazine glamour. I grin, picture high-heels,
matching handbag, silk scarf. A big-hair wig.

No, a straight wig. Voila. Nellie's sequined dress.
Emerald green, full length. Bra sewn in.
I slip it on, get tangled, untangled. Peek out.
Door squeaks open. Freeze-frame. It's Mom.

Barbara West

The first taste of relief I had was during high school

when Cindy's mom decided that all teenage girls should take a rape-prevention class. Our mom agreed this was a good idea, so Cindy, my sister Jennifer, and I enrolled in a series of classes with Karla Grant:

"Ladies, we have today and the next five Saturday mornings to work together. It is imperative that you attend every class.

"On time.

"On a physical level, what I will teach you is tiny—a few, simple but powerful, moves—a fraction of the martial arts repertoire I have spent my life studying.

"But on a psychological level, what we cover will be enormous."

She stopped speaking for a moment, letting us absorb her words from our seats in the basement classroom at UC Davis, twenty or so women and girls, all shapes and sizes, wearing sweatpants and T-shirts. She spoke quietly, without apparent effort, but her voice permeated the silent room. She was tiny, maybe 5'2", with long, wavy, light-brown hair tucked behind her ears. Every motion—her hand making a short chop in the air for emphasis, or the way she paced back and forth in front of the blackboard—exuded strength, power, control:

"The physical techniques I teach you will require practice at home during the week; I am confident that each one of you can master them. But they will not be useful to you unless you address your mindset. No matter how skilled you are, you cannot defend yourself from rape until you address the 'victim tapes' that have been imprinted in women's minds by American culture," her index fingers quickly tapped her temples then offered themselves toward us, palms opening, rotating toward us, offering her gift.

"Ladies, please do not think I partake in 'blame the victim' thinking. Our traditional socialization process teaches women first to be victims and then, secondly, to internalize the blame for their offender's behavior. Just as we are responsible for ourselves, the offender is responsible for his own behavior.

"But in order for us to *not become the next victim*, we must first address the unconscious programming we have received." She tapped her temples again before her hands swung quickly down to rest on the air below her hips like a Wild West hero reaching for familiar holsters. She paused, walked noiselessly across the front of the room. Turned to face us again:

"Several of the techniques I am going to teach you can cause permanent injury to an attacker, or even death. There is no point in learning these unless you are willing to use them, without hesitation, if you are ever attacked."

By this point, we were hardly surprised to find Karla reading our minds:

"If you find you're reluctant to cause permanent injury, or death, to someone who is attacking you, then think instead about what you would be willing to do to defend someone else.

"Think about a child you love.

"What would you be willing to do to defend *a child* from injury, rape, or death?"

She gave us a long pause to think that one over. Jennifer and I flashed on our four-year-old sister Sarah, grinning in her goggles in the backyard pool, learning to swim freestyle that spring ("Big arms Sarah!" "Ice cream scoopers!"). There was no doubt in our minds that we would, without hesitation, maim or kill anyone who threatened her.

Then, the back-and-forth rhythm—between her permeating voice and our unspoken thoughts—gaining momentum, she asked:

"Why wouldn't you do the same for yourself?

"Why aren't you as precious to yourself as that child is to you?"

Cindy, Jennifer and I pondered this all week. We talked it over with our moms. We decided were willing to give it a try—to consider ourselves precious enough to be worth killing for. We weren't sure how that fit with Jesus' teachings. But we already trusted Karla enough to be willing to learn.

* * *

"Today, ladies, you are going to learn the power of your own voice. In order to do this, you will relinquish any ideas you have of properness or 'lady-like' behavior. Let's all stand up now, so we can employ our abdomen's full power."

We pulled ourselves up from our chairs and copied Karla's low, wide stance, one foot slightly forward, toes pointing straight ahead. She had us place our hands on our bellies, our seat of power, she said. She taught us how to draw our breath in down low, which we were proud to already know about, from choir practice. The special shout we would learn—called a *ki-ai*—had to come from deep down inside us:

"A good *ki-ai* is so startling to a would-be attacker, it will likely be the only tool you'll ever need to defend yourself."

Jennifer and I looked at each other, relieved to hear this, because we knew Jesus couldn't have much problem with that. As we turned our faces back towards her, Karla's *ki-ai* hurtled through the basement air, permeated each molecule of our bodies and pinned the soles of our tennis shoes to the cement floor.

It took a beat for our hearts to re-start.

We were terrified.

We were elated.

She had us practice as a group until we could feel our collective shout travel through the steel structure of the building to the uppermost empty floors and through the roof, signaling to the universe that we were irrevocably changed from the compliant young women we'd been when we'd walked in the previous Saturday.

Then Karla had us practice the *ki-ai*, one-by-one, until our last nervous giggle swallowed itself down the well of a deep quiet.

The *ki-ai* was our homework for that week.

Cindy and Jennifer and I got together to practice. It was hard to make yourself do it on your own, even at home with no one there. When you did it right, it seemed that the ceiling might cave in. When you really did it right, it felt very, very good.

* * *

Who could have predicted that six Saturday morning classes would leave a lifelong mark? In the teachings of Karla Grant, feminism and pacifism would meet at a bitter crossroads. When it was over, pacifism would limp into the bushes, nursing a black eye, leaving our valiant sisters in the middle of the intersection, deeply shaken. And stronger.

Where, in her classic 70's feminist way, their mother would remain obligated to take offense at any man opening the door for her, Barbara could now relish this rare recognition of her femininity—while carrying ready keys in her fist, the longest sharply protruding from between clenched knuckles, prepared for whatever, in a midnight parking lot, might await.

Having internalized Karla's teachings, the sisters could then afford to shave their legs and go to the prom. Feminine power had a new grit that refused to be diminished by chivalry, mascara or miniskirts. They had, thanks to their love for Sarah, considered killing.

They practiced their jabs, heel-stomps, and eye-gouges while 300 years of pacifist ancestors looked on from the afterlife in horror. They learned about the anatomical parts that rendered men vulnerable and how to work this to their advantage. After centuries of pounding swords into plowshares, they reversed the process, sharpened shouts into weapons. Chronic, inherited resentment melted into awareness and simple confidence.

A Buddhist might say they took their seat.

The girls each took their own place in the night. They explored the edges of where their bodies ended and others began. Where others ended and they began.

* * *

In a subsequent class, Karla brought up an even more difficult topic: What would you be willing to do to avoid rape?

We'd already decided (sorry, Jesus) we were willing to kill, but now she asked us:

"Would you be willing to die?

"Women are often raped because they believe death is the only alternative. What if you decided you'd rather die than be raped?

"I'm not advocating that point of view," Karla said, as she paced lightly back and forth across the huge classroom, her hair streaming out behind, her tiny body like a big cat on habitual rounds in her too-small cage.

"It's a personal decision only you can make for yourself. And it can change.

"The fact is that most rapists are not murderers. So, adopting an attitude of defending yourself to the death can be a useful psychological tool.

"And, in the rare case of a rapist who *was* planning to murder you, would you rather be raped first or murdered first?

"We have choices here, Ladies! she would remind us again and again."

Karla's words echoed in our minds as we wandered from our lockers to Calculus or Trigonometry. While we pedaled home on the greenbelt, dodging dog-walkers, we felt stretched by the vectors of the new equations she'd laid out for us. We felt a silent *ki-ai* in our core while we practiced dance routines for the high school musical—the quiet, precise brutality of Karla's words liberating us from invisible constraints, sending us forth to tenderly bodyguard ourselves out into the imperfect and dangerous width of this world.

David Dixon

Sisyphus

Perhaps he has invented a game
by trying to land the great rock
in the same place twice.

Just to see.

I imagine him a schoolboy
galloping headlong down
the snow covered hill,
as if next in line for the sled;

and so rise to greet
          another morning.

O' glorious act of the gods!

Steve Cushman

A Missed Shot

My father had been out of the house for two or three months on the afternoon of the basketball game. I still lived with Mom while Dad lived in a piss-yellow trailer off of US 19. When he came to pick me up on Friday nights, I felt as if I were deserting Mom, even though she assured me this was not the case.

My dad wasn't very good at basketball, but played most weekends with a bunch of guys from the print shop where he worked. He always wore a red sweatband around his head, and a matching red wrist sweatband, like he was on the Harlem Globetrotters. I always thought he looked silly. During these games, I stood off to the side of the court, chasing errant passes and tossing the ball back to the players.

It was late in this particular game and I was tired and wanted to go home to my bed and not the lumpy couch in my father's trailer. As I wondered what my mother was doing, my father took a shot and missed. He jumped for the rebound, but one of the other guys bumped him and Dad came down funny. You could hear a pop, even ten yards away; then he was rolling onto the grass, grabbing his ankle.

As I ran over, the other players were helping him up. "Dad, Dad" I said, "you okay?"

"I don't think so," he said.

Smokey, one of the his co-workers who'd been to the house a few times before the split, offered to take him to the hospital, but Dad said he'd be fine. He put his arm around me. His sweat soaked through my T-shirt, wetting my neck and back. When we made it to the car, his old red Datsun B-210, he asked, "Can you drive a stick?"

Where exactly I would have acquired this knowledge at the age of eleven I don't know. As I tried to think of an answer, he winked at me and said, "I'm just kidding."

With him behind the wheel, I ran around and we started for the hospital. Each time he pushed the clutch down, he'd grimace before letting out a little sigh.

"Shouldn't have played that last game," he said. "We should have gone and got some ice cream or something."

"Yeah," I said. "We should have." He'd promised me on the way to the game that we'd stop at Baskin Robbins, but this, like many of his promises, was never fulfilled.

At the ED, he put his arm around me again and we hobbled in. This was before cell phones, so I went over and called Mom from a pay phone, told her we were going to need a ride home.

After Dad returned from Radiology, the doctor came in the room and held the X-ray up to the ceiling light. You could see the break, a thin line through the bigger bone in his ankle. The smaller bone was pushed to the side a little. Even I could tell it wasn't normal.

"We'll reduce the fracture, cast it for six weeks, then you should be fine," the doctor said. This doctor was a big man, stocky, with red hair and two-day stubble. I thought he looked more like a football player than a doctor.

As he held my father's ankle, he asked if we were ready and my father nodded, gripping the sides of the stretcher. The doctor took a long breath in, blew it out, then pulled quick and hard. Again, we heard a pop.

"There you go," the doctor said.

My father turned and winked at me. There was a line of sweat on his forehead, the red sweatband doing its job, drying there in that cool, white hospital room.

"I'm sorry," Dad said.

"For what?"

"For this, hell for everything."

"It wasn't your fault," I said, though I didn't know if he meant my parent's split or for making me late on a Sunday afternoon when I still had homework to do.

Three hours later, Mom drove us home in silence. As she went in and made spaghetti and meatballs, Dad's favorite, he and I sat in the living room, his casted ankle propped up with a pillow on the couch, watching a Celtics-Lakers game on TV. This was during the height of the Larry Bird-Magic Johnson rivalry. Dad was a big Larry Bird fan.

I wanted to tell my father he was tough for driving that stick shift all the way to the hospital, with a broken ankle, but I didn't yet have words for such things. And I didn't know then, and still don't know, why my parents split. In later years, I assumed it was another woman, but I never asked. Some things we're better off not knowing.

When Mom called us in to dinner, I remember my father looking over at me misty-eyed as if he knew this would be the last time he'd be invited to dinner. As if he couldn't believe he'd been lucky enough to live here with his family and foolish enough to lose it all. He opened his mouth to say something but seemed to change his mind as he winked at me instead.

We both sat there for a few moments, not moving, as if that could somehow slow down this moment, and what was happening to our family, make it stretch out forever, or at least a little while longer.

Flying South 2020 Editors

Mary Hennessy (Poetry Editor): Mary was a nurse most of her adult life. She returned to school late and fell in with a community of generous, word-crazed people. Her poems have appeared in many journals and anthologies. One was nominated for a Pushcart Prize and included in the play *Deployed.* One rode the R-bus line in Raleigh. Poetry is the only thing that makes sense to her anymore.

Jennifer Stevenson Vincent (Creative Non-Fiction): Jennifer was twice nominated for the Pulitzer Prize. She has a distinguished career in print journalism, including senior staff writer at the St. Petersburg (Fla.) Times. A founder and past President of Winston-Salem Writers, she's taught creative non-fiction at New York University, the University of South Florida and Salem College.

Bob Shar (Fiction Editor): Bob has been writing short stories for over fifty years -- reading and loving them for over sixty. His stories have appeared in *The South Carolina Review, Greensboro Review, Stoneboat, 2 Bridges Review, Bartleby Snopes, Literary Orphans* and elsewhere. He's a former factory worker, journalist, little magazine mogul (founded/edited/nearly-went-broke-running *The Crescent Review*, 1983-87), two-time Pushcart Prize nominee, retired librarian and village idiot.

Ray Morrison (Fiction Reader): Ray is an award-winning writer whose stories have appeared in numerous journals and magazines, including *Ecotone, Carve, Beloit Fiction Journal, and Fiction Southeast.* He is the author of the story collections, *In a World of Small Truths* and *I Hear the Human Noise* (Press 53).

Steve Lindahl (Fiction Reader): Steve Lindahl is the author of five novels, *Motherless Soul* (ATTMP), *White Horse Regressions* (ATTMP), *Hopatcong Vision Quest* (Solstice), *Under a Warped Cross* (Solstice), and *Living in a Star's Light* (Self Published). His short fiction has appeared in *The Alaska Quarterly, The Wisconsin Review, Eclipse* and others. He served for five years on the staff of *The Crescent Review.*

Contributors

Susan Alff: Susan, of Cary, North Carolina, has studied poetry with Betty Adcock over several years. She placed second in 2000 in the annual poetry contest at NCSU, and had a poem published in English and Russian in *Earth and Soul: An Anthology of North Carolina Poetry*. More recently, she has published in *Wraparound South* and *Flying South*.

Andrew Birkestrand: Andrew lives and plays around Minneapolis Mn with his lovely wife. He washes dishes reluctantly, makes messes exuberantly and tries hair-brained experiments inspired by things he has seen on the internet. He just graduated earning his MFA in Creative Writing at Hamline University in 2019 and has had his short story *On the Day Of* published in 2019 by *Constellations: A Journal of Poetry and Fiction*. He currently works for AmeriCorps, as a literacy tutor in an Elementary school. He learns as much if not more than he teaches in this position.

Kim Bonner: Kim's work has previously appeared in the *Barely South Review*, the *Florida Writers Association Anthology* and her unpublished novel, *Gator Bait* was a 2019 runner up for the Killer Nashville Claymore Award. She is a Florida native and lives happily surrounded by an assortment of rescue animals.

Les Brown: Les is professor emeritus at Gardner-Webb University. His poetry and short stories appear in journals, including *Pinesong, Kakalak,* and *Pine Mountain Sand and Gravel*. His visual art has been featured in journals including *Moonshine Review* and *Broad River Review*. Les, a 2019 Pushcart nominee, recently had his poetry chapbook, *A Place Where Trees Had Names*, published by Redhawk Publications.

Mark Caskie: Mark is a writer and editor who lives in Greensboro, North Carolina.

Steve Cushman: Steve has published three novels. His debut poetry collection, *How Birds Fly*, is the winner of the 2018 Lena Shull Book Award.

David Dixon: David is a physician, poet, and musician who lives and practices in the foothills of North Carolina. His poetry has appeared in *Rock & Sling*, *The Northern Virginia Review*, *Connecticut River Review*, *FlyingSouth*, *Sand Hills Literary Review*, and elsewhere. His first book of poetry *The Scattering of Saints* is forthcoming December 2020.

Deborah H. Doolittle: Deborah has lived in lots of different places but now calls North Carolina home. She has an MA in Women's Studies and an MFA in Creative Writing and teaches at Coastal Carolina Community College. She is the author of *No Crazy Notions*, *That Echo*, and *Floribunda.* Some of her poems have recently appeared (or will soon appear) in *The Coe Review*, *MacGuffin*, *Pinyon Review*, *Rattle*, *Ravensperch*, *Slant*, and in audio format on *The Writers Almanac.* She shares a home with her husband, three housecats, and a backyard full of birds.

Sandra Dreis: As an emerging poet, Sandra works with a critique group of Winston Salem Writers and attends workshops given by NC Writers Network and Press 53. She has enjoyed a terrific, creative summer in Vermont, attending Bread Loaf. For twelve years she taught Drama in the Winston Salem/Forsyth County Public Schools and taught poetry writing for the Arts Connection Team. Her debut YA Fiction, *The Ecowarriors - The Bluffs of Baraboo* received a Silver Nautilus Award (Environmental) in 2016 as well an excellent Kirkus Review. Because she sees life in snapshots increasingly— as she gets older, wiser, her focus is on writing and reading poetry. The recent edition of *Creosote* features her poetry.

Rick Forbess: Rick is a seventy-two-year-old emerging writer with eight published short fiction pieces. His wife, daughter, and he migrated from Texas to Maine almost four decades ago, and here they happily remain. Since retirement from a long career in the mental health field, he has read more, written more, and worked on refining how to approach both.

Lynn Gorski: Born in San Francisco in 1947, Lynn lived in Maryland, Pennsylvania, Alabama, Massachusetts, Maine, Florida, North Carolina and Okinawa - all before her 18th birthday. In 2002 she retired from the Pentagon and moved from Northern Virginia to Charlotte to pursue her personal passion - writing. Since then her *Christmas Story Quiz* and *How Much Do You Know About Easter Quiz* appeared in BRIO Magazine. I have received awards from Charlotte Writers Club and Davidson County Writers' Guild

Joan G. Gurfield: Joan was nominated for the Pushcart Prize. She won the 2018 Short Story Award from *Gival Press*, placed 2nd in the Chattanooga Writer's Guild Contest, was a finalist in the Tucson Festival of Books Literary Awards and the Chester Hines Competition (*Kallisto Gaia Press*), and got Honorable Mention in a New Millennium Writings contest. She has had stories in a *Plymouth Writers' Group anthology*, in *Jewish Fiction*, and in *Milestone*. A longer piece was optioned for a feature film. She has been a professor of English and Creative Writing at East Los Angeles College, arts editor of a small newspaper, and (briefly) a totally incompetent waitress.

Jo Ann Hoffman: Jo Ann's publications include a children's book, short fiction and poems in literary journals, including *The Merton Quarterly, Pinesong, New Verse News, Red Clay Review, Yellow Arrow Journal, Kakalak* and *Flying South*, among others.. She has received contest awards from Carteret Writers, Pamlico Writers and the Palm Beach Poetry Festival. Her non-fiction book, *Angels Wear Black*, recounts the only technology executive kidnapping to occur in California's Silicon Valley. Ms. Hoffman earned her graduate degree in English and Creative Writing from the University of South

Carolina. A native of Toledo, Ohio, she and her husband now live in Cary and Beaufort, North Carolina.

Anthony Howcroft: Anthony's work has been broadly published in a variety of periodicals such as *Ambit, Writers Magazine USA,* and *The London Magazine.* His stories have appeared in numerous anthologies, and his first collection *Nobody will ever love you* was published in 2015. Originally from Oxford, Anthony now lives in America, where he runs a cognitive computing software company.

Earl Carlton Huband: Earl is the author of *The Innocence of Education*, winner of Longleaf Press at Methodist University's 2018 chapbook contest, and of *In the Coral Reef of the Market*, a finalist in Main Street Rag Publishing Company's 2019 chapbook contest, slated to be published by Main Street Rag in July 2020. Both chapbooks are based on Huband's experiences many years ago as a young Peace Corps Volunteer in the Sultanate of Oman, where he taught English in a remote fishing village near the mouth of the Persian Gulf. These poems have been recognized by the Peace Corps Fund for their promotion of cross-cultural understanding.

Porter Huddleston: Porter is winner of the VanderMey Nonfiction Prize, a finalist in the New Millennium Award for Nonfiction, and a current finalist in the OZMA Book Awards for Fantasy Fiction for his debut coming of age literary fantasy novel *El On Earth.* A new writer at the very beginning of his career, he is emerging as a diverse talent as comfortable writing novels and short stories (*Tales My Dad Told Me Before the End of the World, A View of Bea Benton*) as he is penning flash fiction (*The Malcontent, Innocent Blood*) and creative nonfiction (*The Foundation Above Us, What Strange Light the Setting Sun, A Letting of Violet*). His first novel *El On Earth* (unpublished) has been called "utterly unforgettable" by Writer's Digest, a work reminiscent of "Hitchcock scenes shot in the play of light, dark and shadow. Very well done." Early reviews call it "visually haunting and desperately moving." Prior to dedicating himself to writing, Huddleston served as Creative Strategist for

Intel, Managing Editor for Habitat for Humanity International, Proofreader and Business Affairs Liaison for Wieden+Kennedy, and Chief Digital Officer for Brown, Parker & DeMarinis.

Kelly Jones: Kelly resumed writing again last year after a thirty year hiatus. He was recently named as an emerging poet by the North Carolina Poetry Society and a mentee in the Gilbert-Chappell Distinguished Poet Series. He currently works as an arts education supervisor and lives in Tabor City, NC.

Janet Joyner: Janet Joyner's *Waterborne* won the Holland Prize in 2016, and was followed by her *Yellow*, from Finishing Line Press in 2018. *Wahee Neck* was published by Hermit Feathers Press in 2019, which will also release her fourth collection, *Now Come Hyacinths*, in the summer of 2020.

Elizabeth Kirschner: Elizabeth is a writer and Master Gardener, and has published six volumes of poetry as well as an award-winning memoir, *Waking the Bones*. She's currently working on a collection of short stories titled, *Only the Dead Suffer Butter*. Her story, *A Sorry Scheme of Things* is part of this collection. She lives in Maine.

Anne Kissel: Anne, retired from a career in hospice care and elder services, lives in the Chapel Hill part of Chatham County. Becoming 'job free' allowed time to purse a life long interest in writing and to complete the Central Carolina Community College Creative Writing certificate last year. Those classes encouraged her to actually write, instead of just think about writing, and dare to put some of that writing out into the world. Since then she has had poems and short fiction included in the *Red Clay Review*, *Vision and Voice*, *The Mighty Ant*, *Carolina Woman* and *Chat-ham County Silver Arts*.

Marjorie Schratz McNamara: Marjorie never read much poetry until she decided to get a Masters in Creative Writing at NCSU, 30 years after she graduated from college. And she fell in with poets. A good fall. She has been writing poetry for 15 years, been published mostly in NC, and was nominated for a Pushcart in 2016. She lives in Burlington, NC and has enjoyed teaching ESL for years. Garden weeding is her meditation and she is often in transit visiting her far flung family.

Barbara Rizza Mellin (cover artist): Barbara is a painter/printmaker from Winston-Salem, NC. As an art historian, she loves reinterpreting traditional techniques and methods for contemporary audiences. The cover image is a white-line linocut, printed by hand using non-toxic inks. The white-line technique was first introduce in the early 20th century by a group of women known as The Provincetown Printmakers, who wanted to produce multicolor prints using one block. Mellin's art has appeared in juried exhibitions throughout the US, in galleries, universities and museums and internationally online. www.BarbaraRizzaMellin.com

Jaclyn Miller: Jaclyn is married, with four dogs, and lives in Arkansas.

Stanley Moroncini: Stan was in the army for 15 years and served in Iraq and Afghanistan. He was also stationed in Germany and Washington state and much of his writing is based off of experiences in other parts of the world. He has a Bachelors in Business Management and minored in history.

L. G. Pethe: L. G. lives with his wife, Joan, in the Cape Fear region of coastal North Carolina. He currently works as a freelance writer, journalist, and communication consultant. He also is an adjunct college and university instructor in mass communications and film. He earned a bachelor's degree in Journalism from Central Michigan University, and a master's degree in Communication from the University of Notre Dame, with a concentration in prose writing and film. His documentary television writing has been recognized by national organizations, including the New York International Film Festival.

Deborah Phelps: Deborah lives and works in Huntsville, Texas, home of the biggest penal colony and fastest death row in the United States. She has published widely in journals and has a chapbook, *Deep East* (Small Poetry Press, Real Millennial Prize, chosen by Stephen Dunn). Originally from Baltimore, she teaches British literature at Sam Houston State University.

Lian Reese: Lian is a student going into his senior year of high school. He grew up mainly in New York and is now living in South Dakota. This is his first published work.

Joyce Schmid: Joyce's work has appeared in *Literary Imagination, New Ohio Review, Antioch Review, Poetry Daily*, and past issues of *Flying South*. She is sheltering in place with her husband of over half a century in Palo Alto, California.

Trish Sheppard: Trish lives on the coast of North Carolina. She writes, paints and fashions jewelry. Her publishing credentials include: *Shoal Journal, Kyso Flash, Kakalac, Flying South*. Her awards include: 2016, 1st Place Flash Fiction, 2017, 1st Place Flash Fiction & Second Place Poetry, 2018 1st Place Flash Fiction and 3rd Fiction, Carteret Writers Competition. 2017, Honorable Mention, 2018 artist choice poem, Craven Arts Ekphrastic Poetry Contest. 2018, finalist Poet Laureate, North Carolina Poetry Society, 2019, Honorable Mention Palm Beach Ekphrastic Poetry Contest. She also co-hosts three critique groups. The newest one is The Writers Exchange with Jan Parker.

Elizabeth Tarver: Elizabeth is a writer and attorney. She lives in Baton Rouge, Louisiana. Her fiction has appeared in *Image, Berkeley Fiction Review, Beloit Fiction Journal, South Dakota Review*, and other publications. A young adult short story is forthcoming in Zizzle Literary's 2020 Special Edition.

Claire Thomas: Claire currently resides in Asheville and keeps busy from her hodgepodge of jobs ranging from wine bar server to farmhouse caretaker. She enjoys coffee, long car rides and questioning the elusive American Dream.

Landis Wade: Landis is a recovering trial lawyer, award-winning author of books and stories and host of Charlotte Readers Podcast, named Charlotte's Best Podcast, 2019, by Queen City Nerve, where he encourages authors to read and talk about their award-winning, published and emerging works. His third book—*The Christmas Redemption*—won the Holiday category of the 12th Annual National Indie Excellence Awards and was the 2018 Honorable Mention in the 10th Annual Readers' Favorite Awards. The former dean of Wake Forest Law School called *The Christmas Heist*, the first book in the Christmas Courtroom trilogy, a "script somewhere between the screenplays for *My Cousin Vinny* and *Miracle on 34th Street*." As an active participant in the NC writing community, his goal is to use the medium of podcasting to build a community of readers and writers where authors give voice to their written words. For more information about Landis and his writing and podcasting, visit the website: https://charlottereaderspodcast.com/about/

Barbara West: Barbara lives in Davis, California. Her work-in-progress memoir uses mis-rememberings of the movie *Edward Scissorhands* to explore the tension between Christian/Buddhist directives to "help others" and her 12-step Recovery program's directive to "focus on yourself." West is the author of a collection of poetry and prose *...and I felt the simple sweetness of me* (Cold River Press, 2017). Her work has been published in many journals and her performance videos have won awards in film festivals around the world. She works as a wound/ostomy nurse. http://barbara-west.com

Bob Wickless: From Maryland, where he worked as a human resources director for a large, urban police department, Bob moved to North Carolina in 2008. He holds a Bachelor's in English from the University of MD and a Master's in Writing from Johns Hopkins University where he was a Teaching Fellow. His poems have appeared in many magazines and literary journals—*American Scholar, Antioch Review, Poet & Critic, Poetry, Shenandoah, Southern Indiana Review,* and *Southern Poetry Review* among them. A chapbook, *Almost Happy*, recently appeared from Orchard Street Press.

Susan Williamson: Susan is a former newspaper editor, educator, extension agent and a lifelong horsewoman. She is the author of three novels, a children's book, and three how to books. Her latest novel, *Dead in the Loft*, is due to be released in September by Blue Fortune Enterprises. She is currently a contributor to *Next Door Neighbors Magazine* in Williamsburg, VA where she lives with her husband and Labradoodle.

Emily Wilmer: Emily (Alexander, NC) is spiritual director, retreat leader, licensed lay preacher, liturgist, and writer of poems, co-director of Oasis of Wisdom: Institute for Contemplative Study, Practice and Living (www.oasisofwisdom.net). Her poems have appeared in *KAKALAK, Sufi Journal, Thomas Merton Poetry of the Sacred finalist, Great Smokies Review, NC Poetry Society Poetry of Courage award winner (2nd), Flying South 2019, Leaping Clear* and various other journals. Emily received a Pushcart Prize Nomination in 2019. Her chapbook, *Shaft of Light*, will be published in May.

Glenna D. Wolfe: Glenna has been writing all her life. She has published poetry, essays and memoirs, and is currently working on a new book of experiences of a 20th-Century woman. She lives in Chapel Hill with her constant companions, Lucy, the Italian greyhound, and Mattie, the terrier.

Katherine Wolfe: Katherine lives in Goldsboro, North Carolina. She is a retired librarian and a member of the Goldsboro Writers Group. Published works include the memoir *Savannah on My Mind* written with Bettye Clary Toomey and poetry in the *Lyricist, Renaissance, Shoal, Pinesong, Flying South 2017, 2018, 2019* and the Winston Salem Writers series *Poetry in Plain Sight.* Her chapbook *Time That Has Gone* was published by Finishing Line Press in 2018.

Nancy Young: Nancy embraces quirkiness the way some people squeeze puppies. Writing drove her as a reporter, editor, and college educator. She's published articles, stories, poems, three romantic suspense novels (*Seeing Things, Hearing Things, and Sensing Things*), and a poetry chapbook (*The Last Girl Standing*). Occasionally, she wins writing contests.

Pamela Zembiec: Pamela wrote *The Chair* for her daughter a couple of years ago. She was just a baby when her father was killed in Iraq and since that time, Pamela writes to help herself heal. Writing is an amazing form of self-care very effective for the bereavement process. She is currently enrolled in a Master's program through Marian University where she is studying Thanatology. Her goal is to one day teach others to write down their stories to help them heal and grow.

www.ingramcontent.com/pod-product-compliance
Lightning Source LLC
Chambersburg PA
CBHW070608120726
47909CB00007B/2484

* 9 7 8 0 5 7 8 7 2 6 0 1 4 *